I0415672

DEPARTMENT OF THE NAVY
Headquarters United States Marine Corps
Washington, DC 20380-1775

10 December 2004

FOREWORD

The success of any operation depends on proper embarkation planning and execution, whether movement is by land, sea or air. For units to rapidly deploy, commanders must ensure their units maintain the highest degree of embarkation readiness at all times.

Marine Corps Reference Publication (MCRP) 4-11.3G, *Unit Embarkation Handbook*, addresses the doctrine, techniques, and procedures for effectively managing a unit embarkation program and planning and executing embarkation operations. In the case of amphibious embarkation operations, a Marine expeditionary unit (MEU) is used as an example throughout.

The target audience for MCRP 4-11.3G is the noncommissioned officer (NCO) through captain in the embarkation military occupational specialty (MOS) and other NCOs/officers assigned unit embarkation responsibilities.

MCRP 4-11.3G's guidance and relevant information provides commanders and their staffs an appreciation of the internal workings of a unit embarkation section and the critical role it plays in a successful unit deployment. MCRP 4-11.3G serves to provide uniformity across the Marine Corps for integration into standing operating procedures (SOPs).

Reviewed and approved this date.

BY DIRECTION OF THE COMMANDANT OF THE MARINE CORPS

J. N. MATTIS
Lieutenant General, U.S. Marine Corps
Deputy Commandant for Combat Development
Marine Corps Combat Development Command

Publication Control Number: 144 000144 00

MCRP 4-11.3G, UNIT EMBARKATION HANDBOOK

TABLE OF CONTENTS

Chapter 1. Duties and Responsibilities

Chapter 2. Unit Embarkation Program

Chapter 3. Embarkation Automated Information Systems

Chapter 4. Preparing Vehicles, Containers, and Equipment

Chapter 6. Overland Movement

Chapter 7. Sealift

Section I. Amphibious Embarkation Planning

Chapter 8. Airlift

Chapter 9. Redeployment Preparations

Appendices

Tables

Figures

CHAPTER 1
DUTIES AND RESPONSIBILITIES

Embarkation planning and execution is complex. Trained and qualified personnel must be available to perform the host of embarkation duties. Assigning personnel must be carefully done, as embarkation becomes their primary duty during deployment preparations, execution, and redeployment.

The unit commander has overall responsibility for unit embarkation readiness. Familiarity of the following embarkation operations elements and the unit embarkation program provides a baseline of information to address embarkation issues:

- Assigning and training personnel in embarkation duties.
- Embarkation techniques and procedures.
- Force deployment planning and execution (FDP&E).
- Handling, stowage, and transportation of hazardous materials (HAZMAT)/dangerous cargo.
- Movement control procedures during deployment to move cargo from the unit origin (base or camp) to seaports of embarkation (SPOEs) and aerial ports of embarkation (APOEs).
- General characteristics and capabilities of military and commercial transport aircraft and amphibious and commercial shipping.
- Primary APOEs and SPOEs.
- Preparing supplies and equipment for movement by all transportation modes.
- Maintaining the garrison unit deployment list (UDL) in accordance with (IAW) local SOPs.

Unit Embarkation Officer

The unit embarkation officer represents the commander in all embarkation matters. The unit embarkation officer is a Marine officer of any MOS assigned the duties and responsibilities required to ensure the unit can deploy in an orderly and efficient manner. Each unit at the battalion/squadron level should establish embarkation billets on an additional duty basis if not already provided for in the unit's table of organization (T/O). Responsibilities include but are not limited to—

- Keeping the commander informed on embarkation readiness.
- Ensuring adequate orders, directives, and letters of instruction (LOIs) are maintained and published to satisfy all embarkation requirements.
- Creating and/or maintaining a turnover folder and desktop procedures.
- Ensuring reports, load diagrams, and deployment data are correct in content and format.
- Coordinating with the major subordinate command (MSC) embarkation section on any unique policies and procedures.
- Ensuring an embarkation representative is present at ports of embarkation/ports of debarkation (POEs/PODs) during deployments/redeployments.
- Planning and conducting unit embarkation readiness training and inspections.
- Assigning and training personnel for embarkation duties.
- Maintaining knowledge of embarkation techniques and procedures, to include familiarization with the handling, stowage, and transportation of HAZMAT/dangerous cargo.
- FDP&E.
- Understanding movement control procedures used during deployment to support the transport of cargo from the unit origin (base or camp) to the POEs.
- Obtaining knowledge of general characteristics and capabilities of military and commercial transport aircraft, and amphibious and commercial shipping.

- Being familiar with primary APOEs, SPOEs, and PODs.
- Knowing how supplies/equipment are prepared for shipment for all modes of transportation.
- Ensuring the garrison UDL is maintained IAW current Marine air-ground task force (MAGTF) Deployment Support System II (MDSS II) computer-based training instructions, local SOP, and chapter 3.
- Maintaining liaison with appropriate movement control agencies.
- Maintaining unit lift requirements for surface and air transportation.

Unit Embarkation Specialist

Logistics/embarkation specialists (MOS 0431) are assigned down to the battalion/squadron/separate company level. They are formally trained in logistics/embarkation and assist the unit embarkation officer with his duties. Unit embarkation specialists should be capable of fulfilling all MOS requirements as outlined by Marine Corps Order (MCO) 1510.61C, *Individual Training Standards (ITS) System for Embarkation/Logistics Occupational Field 04*. Unit embarkation specialists are responsible for training section embarkation representatives within their unit.

Embarkation Representative

An embarkation representative is normally assigned at the company, battery or section levels and is responsible to the commander or officer in charge (OIC) for the embarkation readiness of the respective company, battery or section. Embarkation representatives can be Marines from any MOS and are usually assigned as an embarkation representative as a collateral duty.

MSC Embarkation Officer

The MSC embarkation officer (limited duty officer [LDO] major [Maj] billet) is available to assist MAGTF and major subordinate elements (MSEs) (regimental or group, warrant officer/chief warrant officer [CWO] billet) embarkation officers. The MSC embarkation officer represents the commanding general (CG) in all embarkation matters. Duties include but are not limited to—

- Serving as the single point of contact (POC) for all embarkation matters.
- Exercising staff cognizance over embarkation policy, procedures, training, and inspections.
- Reviewing subordinate command transportation requests for accuracy and completeness.
- Maintaining liaison with the Marine expeditionary force (MEF) strategic mobility office, adjacent MSCs, subordinate organizations, and external deployment support agencies.
- Verifying Level IV movement data as part of the time-phased force and deployment data (TPFDD) as required. Chapter 5 and appendix A provide details on the TPFDD development process.

Strategic Mobility Officer

A strategic mobility officer (SMO) is an embarkation officer (MOS 0430, LDO lieutenant colonel [LtCol] billet) assigned at the Headquarters, Marine Corps (HQMC), MEF, and Marine Corps forces (MARFOR) levels. The SMO interfaces with the United States Transportation Command (USTRANSCOM) and its subordinate commands as follows:

- Military Sealift Command.
- Air Mobility Command (AMC).
- Military Surface Deployment and Distribution Command (SDDC) (formerly Military Traffic Management Command [MTMC]).

CHAPTER 2
UNIT EMBARKATION PROGRAM

Embarkation personnel must continuously prepare for deployment while in garrison. The unit must be *embark-ready* to deploy safely, orderly, and efficiently.

Turnover Folders and Desktop Procedures

Personnel rotations and reassignments can have a negative impact on unit readiness and day-to-day operations. The impact of personnel turnover is lessened by the proper use of turnover folders and desktop procedures.

All unit personnel assigned to an embarkation billet should ensure turnover folders and desktop procedures are prepared and maintained. Since the majority of the unit embarkation officer/chief duties are synonymous, establishment of a single turnover folder for these billets is permitted. See appendix B.

The unit embarkation officer should maintain a list of specially certified personnel as part of the turnover folder/desktop procedures. This list should identify personnel who are certified in the following courses:

- Certification of Hazardous Cargo for Transportation.
- Aircraft Load Planners.
- Convention of Safe Containers (CSC) Container Certification.
- Nonmanufactured Wood Packing (NMWP).
- Military Customs Inspectors-Excepted.
- United States Department of Agriculture (USDA) Military Cooperation.

Embarkation Reference Material

Embarkation personnel will ensure adequate reference publications and directives are readily available. Readily available is defined as hardcopy on hand, on storage media (3.5 inch disk, compact disk or universal serial bus storage drive) or accessed via an Internet site.

Inspections

Inspections reinforce the importance of combat readiness, evaluate the critical areas essential for mission performance, and are a tool for commanders to assess unit embarkation readiness. Units should conduct an embarkation inspection of subordinate units on a regularly scheduled basis. *The results of the most recent inspection should be maintained in the unit embarkation officer's turnover folder.*

Readiness Assessment Team Visit

A readiness assessment team (RAT) visit is scheduled and conducted by HQMC. The primary goal of a RAT visit is to identify systemic errors at the unit level. Once issues are identified and trend data developed (if any), HQMC can take corrective action to enhance embarkation readiness throughout the Marine Corps. A RAT visit is not a detailed inspection. An embarkation officer, usually a LtCol or Maj 0430 from HQMC's Logistics Plans Office (LPO-3) will be assigned to conduct the visit. If a unit has any embarkation challenges, usually other units are experiencing the same issues or concerns. These areas should be identified to the RAT representative. The RAT visit report is kept internal to HQMC and not provided to commanders.

Commanding General's Readiness Inspection

A commanding general's readiness inspection (CGRI) is scheduled and managed by the Commandant of the Marine Corps, CG MARFOR

(Inspector General), and MEF and MSC inspector staffs. It enables higher headquarters (HHQ) to assess unit embarkation readiness. A CGRI is usually conducted every 2 years IAW local directives.

Logistics Readiness Assessment or Logistics Readiness Inspection

The MSC embarkation officer manages the embarkation portion of the logistics readiness assessment (LRA) or logistics readiness inspection (LRI) program. An LRA/LRI, typically coordinated by the maintenance management officer, consists of inspections within all functional areas of logistics. This assessment provides an indicator of the overall logistics readiness of a unit. The designated MSC representative reports the results to the CG.

Regiment/Group Readiness Inspection

This type of inspection is normally conducted by the next HHQ. It should be conducted at least annually and is recommended before a CGRI.

Staff Assistant Visit

Normally, a staff assistance visit (SAV) will be conducted prior to a formal readiness inspection. A SAV is conducted in the same manner as a CGRI or LRA, but results are not provided to the HHQ in the chain of command. The unit commander will be briefed upon SAV completion. Units request an SAV to their next HHQ.

Battalion/Squadron Level and Below Inspections

Inspections are conducted down to the using unit; e.g., company, battery or section levels. The unit embarkation officer must establish and/or maintain an inspection schedule as part of the unit embarkation program to maintain embarkation readiness per the guidelines established by local SOP. All subordinate organizations to be inspected should be notified via an embarkation inspection schedule/letter and, upon completion,

be provided results to ensure corrective action is taken on discrepancies. See appendix C for sample documentation. Unit embarkation personnel should ensure copies of all inspection results and the action taken to correct identified discrepancies are properly maintained within the unit embarkation officer's/NCO's or embarkation representatives' turnover folders. Inspection results are typically maintained for 2 years.

Embarkation personnel at the battalion/squadron and company levels must have procedures to accomplish inspections to ensure all critical aspects of embarkation readiness can be checked down to the individual section level; e.g., S-1, supply or motor transport.

Company/Section

Inspection procedures are developed to check embarkation boxes, containers, pallet boards, vehicles, and equipment markings, and to update the UDL.

The embarkation NCO will conduct inspections with the embarkation officer, note all problems and correct them in a reasonable amount of time. Companies may request assistance through the embarkation section.

The inspector will examine the stowage designator located on the upper left corner on three sides of the embarkation container, box or pallet board. The item will be measured to determine its cube size. The planned loaded weight will be checked to ensure the correct data is on the UDL.

All vehicles and equipment will be checked for correct markings. The recommended checklist to use for inspections is the MSC CGRI checklist. See appendix D. It will serve to ensure all inspection areas have been considered. The local SOP should be consulted to ensure proper format and content are maintained.

Unit/Section

The embarkation NCO will inspect individual sections on a regular basis. Some pertinent questions are—

- Is there a sufficient number of boxes, containers, pallets/pallet boards, and dunnage on hand to embark the unit's table of equipment (T/E), special allowances, required consumable supplies, and other required non-T/E items?
- Box/container tactical markings (correct weight and cube)?
- Vehicle tactical markings?
- Expeditionary cans?
- Does information on boxes/vehicles match the garrison UDL?
- Does the embarkation NCO maintain a current garrison UDL?
- Is he aware of any changes that may affect the garrison UDL?
- Is the serviceability of all boxes, containers, pallets, and tie-down devices adequate?

Areas Inspected

Inspections should cover administration, management, preparation, automated information system (AIS) proficiency, and the garrison UDL.

Administration

The unit is evaluated on the reference material available, turnover folders, desktop procedures, documentation of unit assessment visits/inspections, and corrective action taken to resolve discrepancies.

Management

A unit should have a sufficient quantity of serviceable embarkation boxes, pallets, pallet boxes, pallet boards, dunnage, banding material, fording equipment, and appropriate procedures for preservation, packaging, and packing (PP&P) of

supplies. A unit basic staging and movement plan to satisfy actual contingency deployment preparations should be in place.

Preparation

All embarkation containers, vehicles, supplies, and equipment will be inspected to ensure tactical and content markings are present and all items are embark-ready. Tactical and content markings are compared against the garrison UDL.

MAGTF II/Logistics Automated Information System Proficiency

Unit embarkation personnel must be inspected on their ability to use the MAGTF II/logistics automated information system (LOGAIS) tools required for embarkation planning and execution. Proficiency tests should include—

- Using MAGTF II/LOGAIS to source a notional exercise or contingency UDL from the garrison UDL and prepare the notional UDL for air, surface, and land movements by assigning carriers and generating transportation control numbers (TCNs).
- Creating exports and imports to and from MAGTF II/LOGAIS and joint AIS to create loading plans. See chapter 3.
- Using automated identification technology (AIT) for UDL management and in-transit visibility (ITV).

Garrison UDL

The garrison UDL audit portion of the evaluation is a critical area that ensures all containers, vehicles, supplies, and equipment are accounted for using the most currently approved version of MAGTF II/LOGAIS. Strict standards for adherence to report formatting and accuracy should be established in HHQ SOPs to develop and maintain deployment data. This data is used to develop deployment plans at the HHQs.

Scale Templates

Since the advent of deployment support AIS, there is no longer a requirement to maintain scale templates for every vehicle or equipment item to accomplish detailed load planning for amphibious shipping or certain classes of Military Sealift Command shipping and AMC aircraft. However, there may be a requirement to accomplish air and sealift load planning *manually* using scale templates *not* contained in deployment support systems' libraries. Sealift templates will be scaled to 1/8 inch equals 1 foot; airlift templates will be scaled to 1/4 inch equals 3 feet.

Reports

MSCs normally establish formats and the type of reports with respective due dates. Sample reports include garrison UDL and the logistics/embarkation billet and training (recommended to be submitted quarterly).

Security Clearances

Secretary of the Navy Instruction (SECNAVINST) 5510.30A, *Department of the Navy Personnel Security Program*, requires a personnel security investigation for personnel who handle sensitive information that, if available to the public, could be detrimental to the security of the United States (US). Since embarkation personnel routinely handle classified information, possession of at least a SECRET clearance is required.

Training

Competent, well-trained personnel significantly contribute to increased readiness and overall efficiency of the unit. All personnel must receive proper formal school and on-the-job training in embarkation-related doctrine, principles, techniques, procedures, and unit requirements. Personnel in embarkation billets should request HQMC-funded formal school embarkation training. Personnel pursuing formal training must coordinate with their respective MSC embarkation section for forwarding of training requirements.

Mission-Oriented Training

Mission-oriented training (MOT) is individual and collective training that provides the Marine with the skills, knowledge, and attributes to discharge duties to support a unit's mission. Unit embarkation officers will ensure, at a minimum, the following MOT is included in the unit's annual training plan:

- Garrison database and UDL file management and reconciliation procedures.
- Refresher training on FDP&E processes to include the annual review of the unit's contingency operation plans (OPLANs).
- Preparing a unit's containers, vehicles, supplies, and equipment for embarkation (to include weighing, tactical marking, and center of balance determination and marking techniques).
- General characteristics and capabilities of military and commercial aircraft, amphibious ships, landing craft, and amphibious vehicles.
- Unit hazardous cargo familiarization/preparation training.

Skill Progression Training

Skill progression training provides a Marine additional MOS skills and knowledge to perform at a higher level. Formal schools, along with ITS for Occupational Field (OCCFLD) 04, form a base of skills progression training that a unit embarkation officer can use to effectively plan for individual and unit training requirements.

MCO 1510.61C provides the unit embarkation officer with a detailed list of those skills required for a Marine within the MOS. Unit embarkation officers should ensure each Marine is given a copy of the ITS and each task completed or skills mastery is properly annotated in his record on a calendar year basis. Unit embarkation officers should conduct ITS training for all 04 MOS personnel on a regularly scheduled basis.

Formal Schools and Mobile Training Teams

Formal school and mobile training team (MTT) courses are offered by Marine Corps Combat Service Support Schools (MCCSSS), Expeditionary Warfare Training Command Pacific (EWTG-PAC), and by other Department of Defense (DOD) agencies. The MSC embarkation section consolidates requirements, publishes schedules, and coordinates embarkation-related training within the MSC. Unit personnel desiring formal school or MTT training should request quota allocations through their MSC embarkation sections. Table 2-1 lists courses available for embarkation personnel.

Table 2-1. Embarkation Formal Schools and MTTs Courses.

COURSE	CODE	LOCATION	DURATION
Basic Logistics Embarkation Specialist	M030D17	MCCSSS	5 Weeks
Landing Force Combat Service Support Chief	M03LBC7	MCCSSS	7 Weeks
Team Embark Officer/Assistant	M030D17	MCCSSS	4 Weeks
Logistics Embarkation Career	M03LAM7	MCCSSS	8 Weeks
Defense Packaging of Hazardous Material for Transportation	AO/C042	Athens, GA	2 Weeks
Transportation and Stowage of Hazardous Materiels	C081	Athens, GA	2 Weeks
Ship loading and Stowage	LAH1	Ft Eustis,VA	2 Weeks
Ocean Terminal and Marine Terminal Operations	LAGG1	Ft Eustis,VA	2 Weeks
Surface Deployment Planning	M7T1	FT Eustis,VA	2 Weeks
Air Movement Planning	N/A	EWTGPAC	3 Weeks
Air Mobility Operations	N/A	HQ, AMC McGuire AFB, NJ	3 Weeks
AMC Affiliation Load Planners	N/A	Designated tanker airlift control element (TALCE)	1 Week
AMC Affiliation Equipment Preparation	N/A	Designated TALCE	2 Days
Intermodal Dry Cargo Ammunition Container	AMMO-L-1O-OS	US Army Defense Ammunition Center & School Savanna, IL (MTT)	3 Days

Correspondence Courses and MOS-Specific Professional Military Education

Correspondence courses and MOS-specific professional military education (PME) provide a Marine with the knowledge base necessary for increased responsibility and professional advancement. Unlike skill progression training, which leads to a specific skill, PME increases overall professional competence in general military education. To enhance professional development of personnel, the unit embarkation officer must ensure the unit's embarkation specialists have enrolled in or completed the following Marine Corps Institute (MCI) correspondence courses:

- Logistics/Embarkation Specialist (MCI 04.5).
- Introduction to Amphibious Embarkation (MCI 04.7).
- Correspondence Procedures (MCI 01.31).
- Marine Corps Directives System (MCI 01.41).
- Math for Marines (1334HP).

CHAPTER 3
EMBARKATION AUTOMATED INFORMATION SYSTEMS

This chapter addresses MDSS II, the embarkation application of MAGTF II/LOGAIS, its procedures, and the joint AIS and load planning tools used in embarkation planning: the integrated computerized deployment system (ICODES) and the automated air load planning system (AALPS). For more information, refer to the current version of MAGTF II/LOGAIS software.

MDSS II has been designed and fielded to facilitate planning in garrison for MAGTF deployments and to interface with the Joint Operation Planning and Execution System (JOPES) through the MAGTF II force planning application of MAGTF II/LOGAIS. Proper use and support of MDSS II is essential to create and maintain a unit's garrison database.

Note: All functions of the current MAGTF II/LOGAIS are planned for incorporation into an enhanced MDSS as the single Marine Corps tool to conduct deployment planning and interface with the Joint Force Requirements Generator II, JOPES, and Global Command and Control System (GCCS).

Unit Garrison UDL

The MDSS II garrison UDL is the source data used to extract exercise or contingency deployment UDLs that define the movement footprint—the unit's lift requirement. The import of a UDL into MAGTF II and the MAGTF II interface with JOPES is the process to develop detailed force deployment requirements. In this way, in conjunction with the MAGTF planners of the unit operations section, embarkation personnel consolidate all unit lift requirements and provide movement requirements through development of TPFDD.

TPFDD provides transportation planners with lift requirements for analysis of the feasibility of movement through POEs/PODs and on to final destinations. For additional information, see the Chairman of the Joint Chiefs of Staff Manual (CJCSM) 3122.02C, *Joint Operation Planning and Execution System (JOPES), Volume III, (Crisis Action Time-Phased Force and Deployment Data Development and Deployment Execution).*

The MDSS II garrison UDL is the source for all other UDLs uploaded into MAGTF II to develop deployment plans, transportation requirements, ICODES/AALPS (ship/aircraft) load plans, and provide ITV to track the throughput of equipment from unit marshalling areas to the final destination during all movement phases. The garrison UDL is active. It requires routine revision, validation, and refinement to ensure that current data is used to develop UDLs and support deployment or contingency plans.

The garrison UDL reflects all authorized unit equipment IAW the applicable T/E and any other authorized special allowances that may be deployed with that unit. All T/E deficiencies and excess items will be reflected.

Developing the garrison UDL will be IAW the MDSS II user's manual/system's help function, local SOP, and the following guidelines.

Mandatory and Required Data Field Entries

Mandatory fields are the serial number and package identification (ID) fields. When records are created, if these fields are not correctly populated, an error code prompts the user to enter the appropriate data before any further entries can be made.

Required fields consist primarily of reference data entries; e.g., unit ID code (UIC), National Stock Number (NSN), and Joint Chiefs of Staff (JCS) cargo category code (CCC). Requiring minimum use of these data fields provides flexibility and facilitates UDL queries via the MDSS II ad hoc report capability.

Level of Detail

The effectiveness of the garrison UDL relies on the accuracy and level of detail of the data it contains. At a minimum, a garrison UDL should be maintained at Level VI detail to accurately reflect its movement requirement.

Garrison UDL Cargo Detail

The garrison UDL will reflect principal end items (PEIs), ammunition, HAZMAT, and other assets to provide visibility of unit capability and enable sustainment requirements determination; e.g., weapons, radios, generators or cryptologic devices.

MDSS II provides an "association" function that links cargo, equipment, and vehicle records to capture how the unit will be configured for embarkation; e.g., placing a box (child) on a pallet (parent) or a pallet on to a truck (parent). As data records are associated, MDSS II automatically updates all its database tables to reflect the combined, as-configured dimensions and weight of affected items.

—————————— WARNING ——————————
When using association, do not change parent record dimensions or weights in a deployment/contingency UDL or garrison UDL because the dimensions and weight information will double. Refer to the MDSS II help function or user's manual for more information.

JCS CCC

The CCC describes the cargo by type; e.g., vehicle, rolling stock, ammunition, container or HAZMAT. This code is arguably the single most important code in UDLs. It provides transportation planners a breakdown of equipment (by type) for movement and sourcing of lift assets. The CCC helps determine the quantity and type of conveyance required and any special handling equipment needed for deployment support.

Deployment Plan Review

Units create a UDL for each deploying unit or detachment for training or contingencies. The garrison UDL is not the unit's deployment UDL—it is the source document from which the deployment UDL is built. Deployment UDLs are created using the embarkation workbench module within MDSS II.

Garrison UDL Audits

Garrison UDL audits should be conducted by unit embarkation personnel (usually done by the embark clerk/NCO) at least on a quarterly basis. This is generally a routine data quality assurance requirement of the MSC embarkation section.

Deployment and Contingency UDL Reviews

MSC/MAGTF commanders will ensure UDLs are validated and adequately reflect the correct information for the actual items scheduled to deploy with the unit/MAGTF that requires transportation support.

AIT

AIT includes the use of logistics applications of automated marking and reading symbols (LOGMARS) and microcircuit technology for logistics applications. AIT is neither a system nor a single product, but a family of technologies that provides a spectrum of capabilities to interface with DOD and commercial information systems. AIT includes but is not limited to bar coding, radio frequency ID (RFID), integrated circuit cards or "smart cards," memory buttons, magnetic strips, optical memory cards, and biometrics. AIT introduces information system efficiencies through the use of enabling technology and standards, providing interoperability not only across DOD but also with our commercial business partners, ensuring a seamless flow of information and goods. For additional information, see MCO P4000.51A, *Automatic Identification Technology Policy Manual.*

Joint AIS

The Marine Corps has enjoyed a reputation among the Services as being a leader in FDP&E. This is primarily attributed to development and use of the MDSS II, MAGTF II, and JOPES/TPFDD interface. The joint AIS and applications listed below allow users to communicate movement requirements to other Services, JCS, and supported and supporting combatant commanders.

Joint Deployment Data Library

The joint deployment data library is a database library that includes standard deployment and transportation fields from a number of authoritative US Government and commercial sources. Standard files include military standard transportation and movement procedures (MILSTAMP), HAZMAT, and equipment characteristics.

ICODES

The ICODES is specifically designed to plan for and execute amphibious, maritime prepositioning force (MPF), and commercial ship loading. It provides advanced artificial intelligence capabilities that assist the planner in making timely and efficient stowage decisions. ICODES planning must first be conducted in MDSS II by assigning the appropriate carriers in the embarkation workbench module, then creating an export file for upload into ICODES.

AALPS

AALPS is designed to create commercial and military aircraft load plans. It can import data from MDSS II and joint AIS for aircraft load planning. AALPS produces AMC-approved load plans. Like ICODES, AALPS planning must first be conducted in MDSS II by assigning carriers using the embarkation workbench module and creating an export file for AALPS.

CHAPTER 4
PREPARING VEHICLES, CONTAINERS, AND EQUIPMENT

This chapter provides guidance to pack, crate, mark, and manifest unit vehicles, containers, and equipment for embarkation. See Joint Publication (JP) 3-02.2, *Joint Doctrine for Amphibious Embarkation*, and Department of Defense Regulation (DODR) 4500.9-R, *Defense Transportation Regulation, Part I, Passenger Movement; Part II, Cargo Movement; and Part III, Mobility*.

The unit embarkation officer will ensure that adequate quantities of the following are on hand for unit deployments:

- Standard embarkation boxes.
- Serviceable crates, pallets, and containers.

The unit is required to maintain sufficient quantitites of dunnage, shoring, banding material, and banding accessories to properly configure embarkation containers and pallet loads. Units maintain sufficient quantities of the above to enable embarkation of all T/E items, special allowances, supplies, and remain-behind equipment (RBE). Garrison property should not be considered for deployment.

Standard Embarkation Boxes, Crates, Pallets, and Containers

Standard embarkation boxes, crates, pallets, and containers will be used to the maximum extent possible. Where practical, use embarkation boxes and containers to store T/E assets in the workspace (reduces overall stowage space).

Standard Publication Box (40 by 16 by 15 inches)

This box has may applications but is primarily used for publications, directives, and unit files. Its compact and lightweight design facilitates mobile loading and palletization of unit cargo and equipment.

Standard Medium Unitized Cargo Box (48 by 40 by 44 inches)

This box is for unitizing equipment, mobile loading, containerization, and 463L pallet building. It fills in for any unit palletized container (PALCON) deficiencies.

Standard Tent/Utility Crate (102 by 42 by 44 inches)

This box is for unitizing equipment, mobile loading, containerization, and 463L pallet building.

Standard Warehouse Pallet (48 by 40 by 96 inches)

Made of a hard wood stringer construction, this pallet was designed primarily for delivery of palletized unit loads by surface or aerial means. The normal load usually does not exceed 2,800 pounds.

United States Marine Corps Standard Container Family

The United States Marine Corps (USMC) standard container family consists of watertight, prefabricated, standard sized, and reusable cargo containers to stow unit property and consumable supplies. These containers are designed to meet shipping and ground transportation standards. They can be handled by an array of materials handling equipment (MHE), tactical vehicles, and transport helicopters.

International Organization for Standardization Container

Twenty-foot International Organization for Standardization (ISO) containers measuring 240 by 96 by 96 inches are maintained in the MEF container pools.

PALCON

The PALCON (Table of Authorized Materiel Control Number [TAMCN] C4431) measures 48 by 40 by 41 inches. It is designed with a standard pallet base, four-way forklift entry, has a cargo capacity of 1,000 pounds, and can accommodate up to six inserts.

Quadruple Container

The quadruple container (QUADCON) (TAMCN C4433) measures 58 by 82 by 96 inches. By its double door entry on both ends, it can be filled with bulk items or fitted with 36 inserts. Maximum load should not exceed 6,500 pounds.

Insert

The insert is designed to fit into a rack within the PALCON or QUADCON to serve as a drawer-bin storage container for supply activities in garrison or the field. It may also be employed separately as a portable, watertight covered field box. The insert measures 45 by 17 by 10 inches and is designed to carry 120 pounds.

Half Container

The half container (HALFCON) (TAMCN C4906) measures 120 by 96 by 96 inches. It is designed primarily for use with the reverse osmosis water purification unit system. Other uses may include mobile loading of hose reels, engines, transmissions, and other oversized cargo. Maximum load weight should not exceed 10,000 pounds.

Water Pump/Storage Module

The water pump/storage module (six containers together [SIXCONS]) (TAMCNs B1580, B1581, B2085, B2086) measures 96 by 80 by 48 inches. It is designed primarily to transport, store, and dispense bulk liquids with the associated pump module.

Tactical Markings

All units will ensure that vehicles, containers, and equipment are marked IAW Marine Corps Forces, Atlantic Order (MARFORLANTO) 4035.2/Marine Corps Forces, Pacific Order (MARFORPACO) 4035.1, *Tactical Marking Procedures for Equipment and Embarkation Containers*. This standardized marking system for vehicles, equipment, pallets, and containers identifies the owning organization, general contents, stowage location, size, weight, and, when required, source and destination of the equipment and cargo.

UIC Markings

UIC markings identify organizational ownership. All units will use UICs to identify their vehicles, containers, and equipment. The UIC marking can be engraved, affixed on a dog tag, embossed on unit equipment or painted on all unit embarkation boxes and containers. Raised letter and number decals obtained through the supply system will be used on vehicles, containers, and equipment painted with chemical agent resistant coating paint in lieu of spray-painting the UIC. See figure 4-1 for placement of markings.

For vehicles, containers, generators, and other items requiring square foot stowage areas, UIC markings will be black, 2-inch, and centered. Where designated marking locations coincide with black paint (camouflage scheme), the marking will be painted earth brown or green.

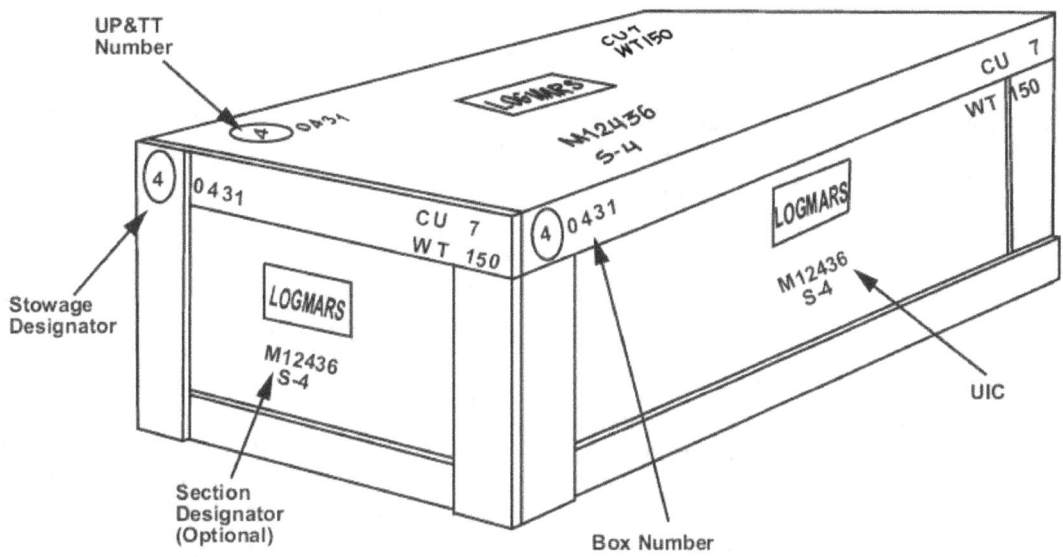

Figure 4-1. Properly Marked Standard Publication Box.

For embarkation boxes, pallets (pallet boards), and crates, UIC markings will be black, 1-inch, and placed on one end, one side, and on the top.

Stowage Designators

A 3-inch white or yellow painted disk (circle) indicates where the cargo is to be stowed aboard ship. Stowage designators are not required on vehicles, QUADCONS, generators or other square foot stowed equipment.

Stowage designators will be placed on each pallet board and in the upper left-hand corner of the top, on one side, and on one end of each embarkation box or crate.

White Disk

A white disk indicates cargo that is hold-stowed on the ship that the owning unit is embarked. However, that cargo does not have to be readily accessible during the ship's transit.

Yellow Disk

A yellow disk indicates cargo that is stowed within the troop office/berthing spaces that must be accessible to unit personnel during transit.

Unit Personnel and Tonnage Table Number

The unit personnel and tonnage table (UP&TT) number categorizes containers by stowage or handling requirements. JP 3-02.2 provides additional information and uses of the UP&TT number. It will be superimposed and centered on the stowage designator in 1-inch black numbers. Appendix E lists applicable numbers.

Package ID Numbers

The package ID number is commonly referred to as a serial or box number and identifies unit vehicles, containers, boxes, pallets, and equipment. It is a required entry in a UDL that enables tracking of vehicles, cargo, and equipment during transit. The package ID number will not be duplicated within the unit.

Vehicles, Generators, and other Items Requiring Square Foot Stowage Areas

The assigned USMC or manufacturer serial number will be used as the package ID number. Package ID numbers will be black, 2 inches high, and placed on the item per applicable technical manuals (TMs). Where no TM guidance is provided, the upper left-hand corners (each side, end, and top) are marked. All vehicles and generators will contain the entire serial number preceded by the letters "USMC." When placement locations coincide with black paint (camouflage scheme), the marking will be painted earth brown or green.

For North Atlantic Treaty Organization (NATO) operations, a solid black five-point star marking will be placed on the front and rear of the vehicle to indicate US ownership. (Per STANAG 2454-AMovP-01A, *Regulations and Procedures for Road Movements and Identification of Movement Control and Traffic Control Procedures and Agencies*.)

ISO Container and QUADCON Markings

ISO containers are marked IAW ISO Standard 6346, *Freight Containers Coding, Identification and Marking*, and ISO Standard 1496-1, *Series 1 Freight Containers-Specifications and Testing*.

ISO containers and QUADCONs are manufactured with two data plates attached. The first data plate contains the manufacturer's contract date, number, and serial number. The manufacturer's serial number is the principal means to track the container in the Marine Corps Supply System. It is used for Defense Transportation Regulation (DTR) codes documentation, developing MDSS II garrison UDL records, and in load planning and templating functions with the joint AIS load planning tools. The second data plate is the CSC safety approval data plate. It contains the date of manufacture, ID number (ISO Registry Number), maximum gross weight, allowable stacking weight, and racking test load value. It also has a

space on its right side to apply the CSC inspection/reinspection decal.

All ISO containers (including Marine Corps T/E items equipped with ISO fittings) must be recertified for serviceability. The manufacturer delivers the container or QUADCON with a 5-year certification. Upon expiration of the initial certification, the unit is responsible to recertify the container or QUADCON.

Details for container operations can be found in JP 4-01.7, *Joint Tactics, Techniques, and Procedures for Use of Intermodal Containers in Joint Operations*, and STANAG 2236, *Multimodal Movement and Transport Matters*-AMovP-5, *Multimodal Transport Issues*. AMovP-5 provides details on ISO characteristics and load planning. It addresses inspecting ISOs, planning loads, packing (to include HAZMAT), and documentation and data plate requirements for use of containers in a NATO operation.

See figure 4-2. Each end of the ISO container or QUADCON is marked in the upper right corner of the right door with the ISO Registry Number. This number is in 4-inch letters/numbers and has a "USMC" prefix. The ISO Registry Number, typically located on the left door, consists of 2-inch letter markings that reflect the maximum gross, tare (empty), and net weights of the container in kilograms and pounds. These markings are required to move the container within the Defense Transportation System (DTS), and must be properly maintained for readability. These markings must **not** be removed or painted over.

The top of the container or QUADCON is also marked with the ISO Registry Number. Both ends of the top are marked in 4-inch letters so they can be read from the nearest end of the container. The UIC markings will be black and 2-inch high as indicated above. When designated locations coincide with black paint (camouflage scheme), the markings may be moved to allow for painting on a contrasting color background or may be painted earth brown or green.

Figure 4-2. QUADCON Markings.

Embarkation Boxes, Crates, and Pallet Boards

Package ID numbers will be 1-inch high and marked on the top, one end, and one side, in the upper left-hand corner to the right of the stowage designator on each box and crate and in the same position for each pallet board. Units will use a unit-assigned four-digit consecutive number system as a package ID number for its boxes, pallet boards, and container markings. For self-contained items with serial number plates (such as AN/PRC-114 radio), the last four digits of the serial number can be used in place of a unit assigned package ID number.

Capability Sets

A capability set is a T/E asset that requires packing or crating of its components in more than one container or pallet, which must be shipped together to maintain its operational capability; e.g., B1226 laundry units. Capability sets may be identified and manifested on the unit's garrison database by using an alpha character following the package ID number; e.g., 001A or 001B.

Cubic Feet and Weight

These markings reflect the cubic foot volume (vol) and weight of each item. When computing the cubic foot and weight, results will always be rounded up to the next higher whole number. The item marking will reflect the rounded number. Cubic feet are computed by multiplying the length, width, and height (inches) of a container or piece of equipment and dividing by 1,728 (Formula: $L \times W \times H \div 1,728 = $ cubic feet).

Vehicles, containers, generators, and other items requiring square foot stowage do not require cubic feet and weight markings.

For boxes, pallets, and crates, cubic feet and weight markings will be 1-inch high, marked on the top, one end, and one side, and placed in the upper right-hand corner.

Expeditionary Cans

Expeditionary cans will be marked with the UIC in black 1-inch numbers, and centered on both sides. If expeditionary cans are black, the marking will be painted in a contrasting color; e.g., white.

Petroleum, oils, and lubricants (POL) cans will be marked with the contents in 2-inch yellow letters on the spout end of the can.

Water cans require only the UIC marking since the word "water" is already imprinted on the sides.

Other T/E Assets

Small items that are mobile-loaded, hand-carried or over-packed in protective boxes or containers should be marked with only the UIC; e.g., night vision goggles (NVGs) and small toolboxes. For small boxes where marking is required and 1-inch markings are too large, smaller markings are authorized.

Administrative Markings

Administrative markings provide amplifying information such as source, content, and destination of the cargo and equipment. Common forms include placarding and labeling.

Placards

Placards provide unit personnel, in-transit agencies, and transportation coordinators with information that expedites handling and throughput of vehicles, containers, and equipment during embarkation/debarkation. See figure 4-3.

```
┌─────────────────────────────────────────┐
│          VEHICLE/CARGO PLACARD           │
│                                          │
│  UNIT LINE NUMBER: _____ │
│                                          │
│  UNLOADING PRIORITY:_____ │
│                                          │
│  LANDING SERIAL: _____│
│                                          │
│  DESCRIPTION: _____│
│                                          │
│  UNIT/SECTION:_____│
│                                          │
│  DRIVER'S NAME: _____│
│                                          │
│  STOWAGE LOCATION: _____│
│                                          │
│  SHIP AND HULL #: _____│
│                                          │
│  REMARKS: _____│
│                                          │
│  HAZMAT:        YES / NO                 │
└─────────────────────────────────────────┘
```

Figure 4-3. Sample Vehicle/Cargo Placard.

Bar Code Labels

Scannable encoded bar code labels provide unit personnel and transportation agencies with an automated means of building databases, conducting inventories, and providing ITV of cargo and equipment.

AIT Labeling

AIT labels provide personnel and transportation agencies with an automated means of building databases, conducting inventories, and providing ITV of cargo and equipment. The appropriate labels or RFID tags must be applied per the references governing the type of movement. Generally, labeling should be applied for each major end item, serialized items (less individual weapon/components; e.g., NVGs or compasses that move separately within a deployment process), vehicles, ISO containers, boxes, pallets or crates. When LOGMARS labels are used, they should be placed 2 inches above the UIC.

Symbolic Markings

Symbolic markings such as unit logos or mascots are **not** authorized.

Packing and Crating

To save stowage space and lessen cargo damage—

- To the maximum degree possible, maintain uniformity in boxes, crates, pallets, and containers.
- Pack like items within the same box/container to facilitate ID and accountability.
- Pad and reinforce containers to protect fragile items and prevent damage to the container and its contents.
- Waterproof boxes or crates containing items subject to moisture damage/deterioration.
- Apply corrosion preventive materials or other appropriate preservatives to items requiring such protection.
- Ensure wood is NMWP-compatible and meets all federal and international standards.

Waterproofing and Corrosion Control

Waterproofing protects those supplies and equipment subject to weather and moisture deterioration during movement.

Plastic Bags

The preferred method of waterproofing is the use of plastic bags and duct tape. Consideration should be given to condensation that may occur through the use of plastic bags. Use of a moisture absorbent material with the plastic bag is highly recommended.

Corrosive Preventive Materials/Preservatives

Before an amphibious operation or when wet landings are anticipated, certain vehicles, equipment, and communications-electronic items will require waterproofing. Use of authorized corrosive preventive materials/preservatives will be applied per applicable TMs.

Palletizing

To prevent damage to embarkation boxes, containers, and equipment during movement, the palletizing techniques listed in Military Handbook (MIL-HDBK)-774, *Palletized Unit Loads,* must be used. Each pallet must be able to withstand inclement weather and rough handling. This pertains to loading equipment on warehouse pallets (wood or metal) and does **not** pertain to 463L pallets. See chapter 8 and DODR 4500.9-R, Part III for further information on 463L pallet loading.

The following guidelines are provided to assist in properly palletizing a unit's standard cargo containers, boxes, and equipment. See figure 4-4.

- Maintain a sufficient quantity of serviceable standard pallets on hand for all supplies and equipment that will be embarked or remain behind in storage.
- Pallets will have four-way forklift access for loading and handling.
- Pallets will have a stringer construction with a 4-inch overhang on both ends for using lifting slings during crane on/offloading.

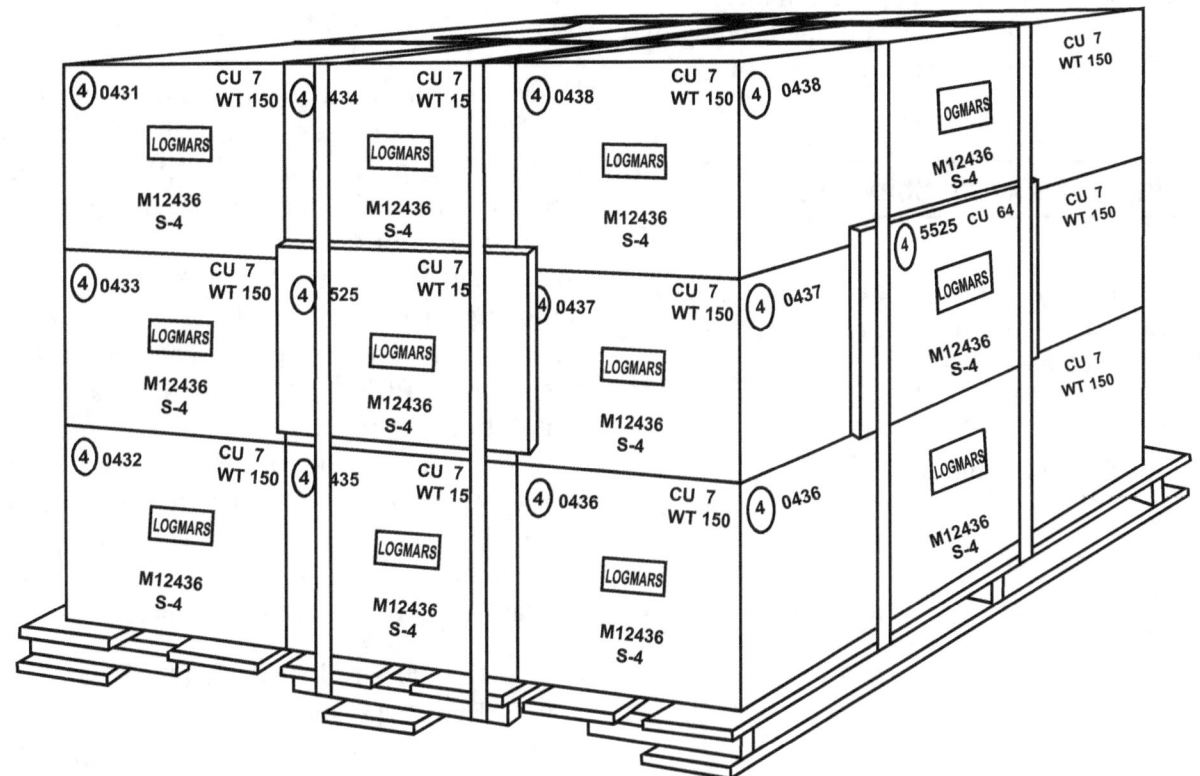

Figure 4-4. Warehouse Pallet Load.

- Pallet construction will include banding recesses for the banding straps. Place banding straps through the slots on the pallet stringer so they do not interfere with forklift tines.
- Use only 1 1/4-inch banding when palletizing cargo. Band in both directions to ensure the load is secure.
- Pallets will be squared off as much as possible to allow stacking or overstow. Depending on their weight, pallets may be stacked three high during staging and while in transit. A 40-inch height is recommended for maximum stowage of pallets. However, 52 inches is considered to be the maximum height allowable for unitized cargo while embarking aboard amphibious shipping and should not be exceeded.
- Maintain three pallet boards for each pallet. The pallet board will be of sufficient size (not to exceed 12 by 18 inches) to accommodate all required markings.
- Tentage and poles not used for on-going field operations will be palletized and or crated in garrison to maintain embarkation readiness.
- Band expeditionary cans to pallets in three rows of seven. Care must be taken in the banding of plastic expeditionary cans to prevent damage.

Preparing HAZMAT for Shipment

Units often overlook packing and packaging of hazardous cargo. All units use and often embark HAZMAT such as—

- Explosives.
- Flammable liquids and solids.
- Oxidizers.
- Corrosive materials.
- Compressed gasses.
- Poisons.
- Irritating materials.
- Etiologic agents.
- Nuclear, biological, and chemical (NBC) defense testing and neutralizing substances.

- Commercial lantern fuel; e.g., Coleman™.
- Cleaning agents.
- Lithium batteries.
- Radioactive materials and other regulated materials and substances whose properties can be considered dangerous.

Units will review supplies and equipment on hand, those planned for embarkation, and identify those known to be HAZMAT. Any questionable items will be identified to the embarkation section for guidance on packaging and handling/shipping instructions.

Items identified as hazardous are required to have the proper HAZMAT ID labels placed on three sides of the container for shipment. This ID label is used to assign the stowage location aboard the designated transportation asset (ship, aircraft, truck or rail). Title 49 *(Transportation)* of the Code of Federal Regulations (CFR) provides specific requirements and shows label examples.

Embarkation personnel (0431 NCO per the current ITS) must be certified in preparing HAZMAT for shipment to ensure that unit hazardous cargo has been properly identified, packed, packaged, and certified for transportation. HAZMAT certifiers will use a generic Shipper's Declaration for Dangerous Goods format to document hazardous cargo. The format describes the HAZMAT and provides handling information; e.g., some HAZMAT cannot be moved on a passenger aircraft so the format would have "Cargo Aircraft Only" annotation, where required. This would affect load planning to adjust loading of an aircraft without personnel. Units are required to have MCO P4030.19H, *Preparing Hazardous Materials for Military Air Shipments*, readily available. Additional references include—

- DODR 4500.9-R, Part II, chapter 204.
- CFR Titles 46 (*Shipping*) and 49.
- International Maritime Organization (IMO) International Maritime Dangerous Goods (IMDG) Code.

- NATO STANAGs.
- International Air Transport Association (IATA) *International Standards and Recommended Practices* and/or International Civil Aviation Organization (ICAO) regulations.

DD Form 1387-2, *Special Handling Data/Certification*

See figure 4-5. Per DODR 4500.9-R, Part II the shipper (unit movement or traffic management personnel) must complete DD Form 1387-2, *Special Handling Data/Certification*, for all cargo and equipment identified with special characteristics and handling requirements regardless of the mode of transportation. An example may be the S-2 intelligence section wants to ship a three-drawer combination safe. The embarkation representative would ensure that a DD Form 1387-2 is completed and attached to the safe to track it through transit. The DD Form 1387-2 will inform all concerned in the DTS of the requirement to ensure the safe is secured at all times. The DD Form 1387-2 is considered an additional shipper documentation requirement.

Note: DD Form 1387-2 is no longer used to certify HAZMAT.

Recommended Embarkation Supplies and Equipment

Embarkation supplies and equipment must be readily available to conduct short notice embarkation operations and provide the unit with the equipment to train its personnel. See appendix F. Typical uses of the most important items follow.

ITEM NOMENCLATURE | NET QUANTITY PER PACKAGE | TRANSPORTATION CONTROL NO.

CONSIGNMENT GROSS WEIGHT | DESTINATION

SUPPLEMENTAL INFORMATION | LOAD STORAGE GROUP | FLASH POINT

This is to certify that the above named materials are properly classified, described, packaged, marked and labeled, and are in proper condition for transportation according to the applicable regulations of the Dept of Transportation. THIS IS A MILITARY SHIPMENT! *(Complete applicable blocks below)*

- This shipment is within the limitations prescribed for PASSENGER AIRCRAFT/CARGO AIRCRAFT ONLY (Delete nonapplicable aircraft)
- AFR 71-4, TM 38-250, NAVSUPPUB 505, MCO P4030.19, DLAM 4145.3, Paragraph ______
- DOD 4500.32R (MILSTAMP)

ATA/IATA/IMCO REGULATIONS		
	PARAGRAPH	EXEMPTION
49 cfr	173.7(a)	DOT-E 7573

ADDRESS OF SHIPPER | TYPED NAME, SIGNATURE AND DATE

DD FORM 1387-2, JUN 86 *Previous editions are obsolete.* *Form Approved/OMB No. 0704-0188*

SPECIAL HANDLING DATA/CERTIFICATION

Figure 4-5. DD Form 1387-2, Special Handling Data/Certification.

Banding Wire and Banding Tools

Units should maintain a minimum of two sets of crimpers, cutters, stretchers, and a sufficient quantity of 1 1/4-inch steel banding wire and clips to meet the unit's pallet building and overall embarkation requirements. A nylon or plastic banding wire system can be substituted if it can safely secure the pallet load.

Tool Kit

Unit embark personnel should have hammers, nails, pliers, saws, and various screwdrivers readily available during embarkation.

Tape Measure and Calculator

Each embarkation representative should have a tape measure and calculator to determine and verify square foot and cube requirements and dimensions of vehicles, cargo, and equipment.

Portable Wheel Scales

Each unit should be authorized (check the unit T/E) to possess scales to weigh and determine the center-of-balance of unit vehicles, cargo, and equipment.

Administrative Supplies

The unit embarkation section should maintain enough supplies to conduct a unit move. Examples include—

- Airlift/sealift placards.
- Document protectors.
- Staple guns/staples.
- Grease pencils.
- Chalk.
- Duct tape.

- 1-, 2-, and 4-inch stencil sets.
- Spray paint.
- Waterproofing materials.

Safety Equipment

Each unit should maintain a sufficient quantity of safety equipment to meet mobility requirements. At a minimum, each embarkation representative should maintain the required personal protective safety equipment. Safety equipment should at a minimum include plastic hard hats, safety boots or boot caps, work gloves, ear/eye protection, and flashlights with wands and lens filters.

Special Ramps and Lifting Slings

Unit embark sections should maintain special ramps and or lifting slings to support loading requirements; e.g., ramps for loading helicopters aboard transport aircraft and slings for 155 millimeter [mm] howitzers.

Tie-Down Material (1/2-inch Rope/Cargo Straps)

Units should maintain tie-down material to secure mobile loads. Sufficient quantities of 1/2-inch rope or 500-pound capacity cargo straps should be maintained within each unit to accommodate all planned mobile loads for contingency and routine deployments.

Padding and Reinforcing Materials

A sufficient quantity of padding (bubble wrap) and reinforcing materials should be maintained within each unit to pack its supplies and equipment requiring such protection.

Vehicle Preparation

The term "vehicle" pertains to trucks, trailers, fork-lifts, road graders, bulldozers, tanks, amphibious assault vehicles (AAVs), light armored vehicles (LAVs), and other rolling stock and tracked equipment. To ensure all vehicles are prepared for embarkation, the following tasks must be accomplished:

- Check engines, fuel lines, and mobile-loaded fuel cans for leaks. Ensure any defects are corrected before moving to embarkation points.
- Vehicles are clean, to include engine compartments, tracks, road wheels, and under carriages.
- Vehicles are at full operational capability.
- Based on the mode of transportation, bows for canvas tops are removed from cargo compartments and attached to the vehicle's body. Canvas tops are folded and placed in the vehicle storage compartment, when required. Exhaust stacks/tire racks are removed and placed in the bed of the vehicle to reduce vehicles to their minimum height.
- Identify in advance all cargo to be mobile-loaded.
- Stow mobile-loaded cargo no higher than the highest fixed point of the vehicle (no higher than the cargo compartment side-rack unless containerized in a QUADCON or other type storage container).
- Inspect vehicles and trailers to ensure lifting points, shackles, and pintle hooks are in ser-

viceable condition. All lifting shackles/pintle hooks must have cotter pins regardless if the vehicle has a towed load associated to it.

- Embark vehicles with fuel tanks filled not to exceed 3/4 of a tank-full. However, depending on the mode and location of the vehicle on a particular mode of transportation, there may be a specific fuel limitation according to the applicable loading manual.
- Secondary loads are mobile loads carried in the vehicle cargo compartment or bed. Mobile loads may be individual equipment or supplies properly palletized on a standard warehouse pallet. Secure secondary loads to the vehicle with a minimum of 1/2-inch rope, cargo straps or chains, and tie-down devices.
- Determine an accurate vehicle weight during embarkation planning. Each mode of transportation has its own specific weight restrictions. Vehicles must be mobile-loaded so they do not exceed cross-country weight limitations, thereby avoiding frustrated cargo at staging areas and APOEs/SPOEs. Chapters 6 through 8 cover the specific weighing and marking procedures for overland, sealift, and airlift transportation of vehicles.
- The unit is responsible for providing all approach, rolling, parking, sleeper shoring, dunnage, chocking, and blocking and bracing material for safe containerization and loading and transport of vehicles, supplies, and equipment.

CHAPTER 5
FORCE DEPLOYMENT PLANNING AND EXECUTION

The Marine Corps developed the FDP&E methodology to better plan command and control (C2) for deployments. MAGTF commanders wanted a single source of timely deployment information to identify force requirements and ensure that associated deployment plans supported the concept of employment. They also wanted to present consolidated movement requirements to the combatant commander, joint force commander, and the Commander, USTRANSCOM. FDP&E provides a means to monitor and influence the flow of MARFOR and associated warfighting capabilities into an area of operations (AO).

FDP&E describes the methodical oversight of deployment plan/TPFDD creation, plan management, and plan execution using standardized policies, guidelines, procedures, and formats. It is a combination of the operations and transportation planning procedures used in deliberate and crisis action planning for mobilization, deployment, employment, sustainment, and redeployment. FDP&E includes the execution of those plans through the deployment of forces and their subsequent sustainment to support the concept of operations (CONOPS).

TPFDD

TPFDD is a component of JOPES, an integrated joint C2 system that supports military operations planning, execution, and monitoring activities. JOPES incorporates policies, procedures, personnel, and facilities by interfacing with automated data processing (ADP) systems, reporting systems, and underlying GCCS ADP support.

JOPES provides senior-level decisionmakers and their staffs with an enhanced capability to plan and conduct joint military operations. See CJCSM 3122.02C, *Volume III*, and appendix A for more information on TPFDD.

Normally the MSC and HHQ G-5/JOPES cell will publish a TPFDD LOI for the development of force movement requirements, the sourcing of forces to fulfill identified requirements, and the deployment and redeployment of those forces.

Transportation Planning

Meeting the required arrival dates of personnel, vehicles, supplies, and equipment at the intended destinations is the ultimate goal of transportation planning. It involves determining the throughput requirement; i.e., the who, what, when, where, and how personnel and materiel must move to support the TPFDD and sustain the force.

Transportation planners express initial force movement requirements in terms of tonnage, number of personnel, and distance. As detailed planning continues, tonnage is quantified by classes of supply or PEIs. Distances between specific origins and destinations become movement legs. Transportation planners estimate requirements based on the supplies needed to support the MAGTF and the average distances to move during each phase of an operation. For dedicated airlift, 100 passengers (PAX) or 15 short tons (S/Ts) is the minimum planning requirement for a unit line number (ULN) movement. This estimate provides a starting point to develop and refine the TPFDD.

Force Movement Requirements

Force movement requirements are the personnel, vehicles, supplies, and equipment to be moved, derived from the UDL and personnel data uploaded into JOPES (TPFDD) through MAGTF II. Data is sequenced by required delivery date (RDD) and priority within the RDD. These requirements must be accurately sourced by deploying units and identified at a minimum of TPFDD Level IV detail before the MAGTF commander passes the consolidated requirement to the combatant commander for validation. The combatant commander submits them to USTRANSCOM for sourcing of the appropriate transportation assets.

Lift Mode and Source

The selected lift mode and source identifies what transportation means move a specific ULN between each movement leg; e.g., between point of origin (camp, base or station) and POE, POD or destination (assembly area). Refer to the HHQ TPFDD LOI for specific mode and source definitions.

POE

The POE is the geographic point in a routing scheme where cargo or personnel depart; e.g., a Camp Pendleton unit embarks out of Naval Station (NS), San Diego aboard amphibious shipping. The POE is NS, San Diego, the origin is Camp Pendleton. This may be a seaport or aerial port where personnel and equipment flow to a POD. For unit and nonunit requirements, it may or may not coincide with the origin.

POD

The POD is the geographic point where cargo or personnel are discharged. This may be a seaport or aerial port; for unit requirements, it may or may not coincide with the destination.

Timing

Transportation planners must consider—

- RDD at the destination.

- Ready-to-Load Date (RLD): the day relative to C-day when unit and nonunit equipment and forces are prepared to depart their origin on organic transportation or are prepared to begin loading on USTRANSCOM-provided transportation.
- Available-to-Load Date (ALD): a day relative to C-day when the unit or nonunit equipment and forces can begin loading on an aircraft or ship at the POE.
- Time/distance factors between the point of origin, POEs, PODs, and final destination.

Throughput

Throughput is the average quantity of cargo and PAX that can pass through a port on a daily basis from arrival at the port to loading onto a ship or plane or from the discharge from a ship or plane to the exit (clearance) from the port complex. Throughput is usually expressed in measurement tons, S/Ts or PAX. Reception and storage limitation may affect final throughput. Port throughput data should consider not only port offload capability, but also the theater's ability to move and sustain forces away from the port. Matching the strategic TPFDD flow to the theater's reception, staging, and onward movement capability should prevent port saturation and backlogs that slow the buildup of mission capability.

Force Protection

Force protection encompasses the security of POEs and PODs, advance or intermediate staging bases, and supply depots.

Special Requirements

Transportation planners must consider—

- Permits needed for oversized loads.
- Routing considerations due to bridge capacities.
- Impact of terrain, climate, and the environment.

Determining Resources

Transportation planners must consider—

- Characteristics and capabilities of commercial and military modes of transportation.
- The capabilities of host nation transportation and deployment support.

Coordination

Constant coordination by transportation planners with operation planners is necessary to accommodate changes in the MAGTF commander's CONOPS, lift requirements, movement priorities, and allocations of transportation assets.

Selecting the Unit Marshalling Area

A unit marshalling area is a centralized location large enough to stage personnel, vehicles, supplies, and equipment to be organized and prepared for movement. If space is limited, a movement schedule must be established to phase the movement of personnel and assets through the marshalling area. Doing so will ensure the embarking unit can meet inspection and deployment timelines.

Accessibility

The marshalling area should have entry and exit points to accommodate moving vehicles and MHE through the area.

Lighting

Lighting should be available to accommodate work at night. If lighting is not available but required, then requests for floodlight sets should be submitted.

Portable Toilets

Marines must have appropriate sanitary facilities to support 24/7 operations. Proper coordination must be made with the base operations support group/station operations support group via HHQ for portable toilet support.

Water Points

Water is required to hydrate Marines supporting marshalling operations and may be required to conduct agricultural washdown operations.

Medical Support

Medical support should be coordinated with embarking unit aid stations. Corpsmen should be at the marshalling area when conducting operations.

Marshalling Area Workspace

Embarkation or logistics personnel should coordinate a marshalling area workspace. The workspace may be a tent or an existing building. It should provide embarkation, movement control, and administrative personnel sufficient office space and support capability to conduct MDSS II deployment database management, passenger manifesting, convoy assignments, communications (land line and e-mail), and any additional administrative requirements.

Communications Support

Communications support should be coordinated with the embarking unit's communications section (S-6). Operations may require e-mail connectivity, telephone lines (land lines and cellular phone support), very high frequency radios, and hand-held radio support.

Security Force

A security force will be required to protect gear from pilferage, specifically if any sensitive gear is pre-staged overnight or if called for by the current force protection threat condition. Security will be a key consideration of the MAGTF commander and his staff force protection officer.

Organizing the Marshalling Area

The marshalling area should be organized to prepare unit equipment for movement and correct any discrepancies identified in equipment/vehicle inspections. Often, the marshalling area will be shared with administrative personnel to process and manifest personnel for transportation. Some areas needed within the marshalling area follow.

463L Pallet Buildup Area

The 463L pallet buildup area should be large enough to accommodate all the unit's cargo and baggage required to deploy by air. The area needs to be able to stage each 463L pallet on three pieces of dunnage. Additional room should be allocated to allow the use of MHE to access the pallets.

Mobile Loading

This area should be large enough to accommodate the staging of unit vehicles, equipment, and supplies required to be mobile-loaded and provide room for MHE operations.

Vehicle Staging

Vehicles should be parked so any vehicle can be moved without moving anything else while maintaining unhindered access to the exit point.

Personnel Processing Station

This area is usually located within the marshalling workspace and may require additional desks and chairs for administrative personnel. It should be separated from any cargo and vehicle movement as much as possible and provide sufficient space for passenger manifesting.

Vehicle Loading Area

This area should be large enough to accommodate buses and tractor trailers and located near the exit point. It must be located near a loading ramp to load rolling stock onto flatbed trucks.

Required Equipment

All items required to prepare supplies and equipment should be on hand. Supporting equipment may include—

- MHE.
- Portable wheel scales.
- 463L pallets, side and top nets, waterproof bags, shoring, and dunnage.
- Tie down material/devices.
- Other waterproofing material.

Unit Marshalling Area Diagram

A diagram should be drawn (to scale if possible) that reflects the areas, support, and flow through the marshalling area. Copies should be given to all Marines associated with the movement within the marshalling area.

Movement Control Agencies

Embarkation personnel should be familiar with movement control agencies and their functions at all levels.

MARFOR Headquarters Movement Control Center

This movement control center (MCC) keeps the commander, Marine Corps forces (COMMARFOR) informed of the status of subordinate unit movements. It also coordinates and prioritizes force deployment requirements with USTRANSCOM.

Force Movement Control Center

During a major deployment, the MEF commander will activate a force movement control center (FMCC), a logistics and movement control center (LMCC), and a flight ferry control center (FFCC) to coordinate all strategic, operational, and tactical lift requirements for land and air forces. The FMCC is normally staffed by members of the MEF component assistant chief of staff (AC/S) G-4 (SMO) and will coordinate

FFCC operations for air forces and LMCC operations for land forces. The FMCC will coordinated all strategic lift to move the forces from the APOEs and SPOEs to the aerial ports of debarkation (APODs) and seaports of debarkation (SPODs), and will facilitate LMCC representation at the theater joint movement center.

LMMC

The LMCC is resident in the force service support group/combat service support element (FSSG/CSSE). It is the executive agent for the MAGTF commander's movement, coordination, and control. The LMCC provides Marine Corps organic and/or commercial transportation, transportation scheduling, MHE, and other support during marshalling and movement. The FSSG/CSSE can also establish the arrival/departure airfield control group (AACG/DACG) and the port operations group (POG) as subordinate to the LMCC. One or more of each group may be required; e.g., if a unit is deploying via strategic air from two airfields, two AACGs would be required.

AACG/DACG

The FSSG/CSSE provides an AACG/DACG under the operational control of the LMCC. The AACG/DACG provides the interface between the deploying force and the AMC TALCE. Its mission is covered in detail in DODR 4500.9-R, Part III and MCWP 4-11.3, *Transportation Operations*.

POG

The FSSG/CSSE establishes a POG under the operational control of the LMCC. The POG provides control, coordination, and support at designated SPOEs/SPODs. POGs provide traffic control, MHE, and stevedore support for loading ships.

Railhead Operations Group

The FSSG/CSSE may establish a railhead operations group (ROG) under the operational control of the LMCC. The ROG will provide the expertise in loading and securing equipment on different types of railcars. They also provide traffic control and coordination at the railhead.

Airlift Liaison Element

The deploying unit commander establishes an airlift liaison element (ALE) at the airhead to coordinate between the deploying unit and the AACG/DACG.

Sealift Liaison Element

The deploying unit commander establishes a sealift liaison element (SLE) at the port to coordinate between the deploying unit and the POG.

MSC Unit Movement Control Centers

MSC commanders control organic transportation and communications assets and coordinate with the LMCC to execute deployments. On order, each command activates its unit movement control center (UMCC) to support marshalling and movement to APOEs/SPOEs. Depending on their geographic locations, some MSCs may choose to operate a readiness movement control center, which is similar to an MSC UMCC.

Organizational UMCCs

Every deploying unit down to the battalion, squadron or separate company level activates a UMCC to control and manage its marshalling and movement.

Base Operations Support Group and Station Operations Support Group

Bases and stations establish operations support groups to coordinate their efforts with those of the deploying units. Like Marine Corps base commands, most air stations have transportation, communications capabilities, and other assets and support useful to all commands during deployment.

FFCC

In addition to its UMCC, the Marine aircraft wing (MAW) establishes an FFCC to support and monitor movement of organic deploying fixed-wing aircraft. The center operates under the cognizance of the MAW, operations section (G-3).

CHAPTER 6
OVERLAND MOVEMENT

Overland movement is an integral part of strategic mobility, embarkation, and deployment operations. It is the movement of unit vehicles, rolling stock, equipment, and supplies from staging or unit marshalling areas to the APOE/SPOE for loading aboard aircraft or shipping IAW the unit embarkation plan for further transport to the designated AO. Once in the AO, overland movement and requests for overland transportation support must be coordinated via the designated US theater support organization, host nation support agreements or organically within the MAGTF to ensure unit equipment moves as scheduled from the APOD/SPOD to the tactical assembly areas.

Transportation Modes

All units should examine their deployment requirements and follow the transportation planning process described in chapter 5. Units must consider using organic assets first when determining their transportation requirements. Any requirements beyond the unit's organic capability should be identified as early as possible to HHQ so external support can be coordinated expeditiously.

The number of personnel and the volume of freight generally combine to define overland movement requirements. These requirements can be satisfied using commercial buses, trucks or rail. Unit movement planners should contact their local LMCC/transportation management office (TMO) to determine current costs for each type of commercial transportation mode/carrier available. Capturing these costs is critical to documenting movement costs associated with exercise or contingency transportation budgets and forecasting future requirements. Each mode has a

specific capability to support unit movement. See appendix G for general capabilities of each mode.

Marine Corps Motor Transport Assets

The Marine Corps has a wide range of tactical vehicles used during day-to-day operations to satisfy units' external overland transportation requirements. Transportation support battalion has the bulk of these assets to support the resident MEF. These vehicles range from high mobility, multipurpose, wheeled vehicles (HMMWVs) to the heavy lift, logistics vehicle system (LVS). See figure 6-1. Marine Corps TM 11240-15/4C, *Motor Transport Technical Characteristics Manual*, lists fielded motor transport assets.

Figure 6-1. LVS MK-48 Power Unit/ MK-14 Powered Trailer.

Commercial Buses

Normal planning capacity is 45 to 47 PAX per bus. Buses have limited baggage capability in cargo bays under the bus and should not be used to transport cargo; e.g., seven-cube boxes, desktop computers or NVGs.

Commercial Trucks and Trailers

Various types of commercial freight modes are ordered by the LMCC/TMO to move unit equipment. The modes needed depend on the type and configuration of unit containers, equipment, and supplies; e.g., a heavy equipment transport would be required to transport an amphibious assault vehicle, personnel (AAVP)-7 or an M1A1 tank. Commercial trucks move personal baggage, embarkation boxes, PALCONs, QUADCONs, and unit vehicles. Typical commercial trucks ordered are—

- Standard flatbed trailers (45 to 48 feet) to move standard embarkation boxes, PALCONs, QUADCONs or ISO containers. See figure 6-2.
- Standard low-bed trailers normally used for LAVs, AAVs or trucks mobile-loaded with maintenance vans or shelters.
- Standard enclosed trailers (48 feet), normally used for baggage or bonded cargo.
- Explosive trailers. All HAZMAT/explosive ordnance trailers are coordinated through the base or station TMO. State highway requirements and Coast Guard class of hazards will dictate the type of commercial assets needed.

Figure 6-2. Flatbed Trailer with QUADCONs.

Rail

Commercial and DOD rail are used in transporting heavy lift requirements or when moving units long distances to produce a cost savings in lieu of using commercial trucks.

Bi-Level Car

The bi-level car is normally used to transport HMMWV variants. It is designed to hold a total of ten vehicles (five on the top deck and five on the lower deck) with a height restriction of 76 inches on the lower deck. Top deck height restrictions are based on overpass clearance requirements peculiar to the route between the departure and arrival railhead.

DOD-Owned Railcars

DOD-owned railcars (DODX) are positioned at various bases to support movement of oversized equipment (M1A1 tank or AAVs) for training or contingencies. Most cars measure 89 feet (normally referred to as "89 footers"), and have a wooden deck.

Flatbed Cars

There are two types of flatbed cars, also referred to as "89 footers".

- Steel decked, which transport a wide variety of wheeled assets.
- Wooden decked, which specifically transport steel tracked assets, such as bulldozers.

Container Cars

Container cars are specifically designed to carry four standard 20-foot ISO containers. They can also transport QUADCONs when they are locked together in a group of four using the locking device designed for QUADCONs.

Request Procedures

Timeline

Typically, each type of commercial transportation conveyance will have different timelines for requesting support. Local SOP and availability of commercial assets will ultimately dictate request submission timelines. Typical commercial timelines will assist the overland movement planner in requesting support.

Typical Commercial Bus Request Timelines

- Optimal request submission: 7 working days before movement date.
- Minimal request submission: 48 hours before movement date.

Typical Commerical Freight Request Timelines

- Optimal request submission: 15 working days before movement date.
- Minimal request submission: 7 working days before movement date. *Exception: explosive ordnance movements normally require a minimum of 10 days lead-time. Check local SOP.*

Format

The format for submitting external transportation support requests is determined at the local level. Transportation of things/transportation of people (TOT/TOP) request procedures vary from base to base and are normally determined by the LMCC or base TMO. Review local LMCC procedures to determine correct format. Appendices H and I are examples of data required for most TOT/TOP requests.

On/Offload Time Constraints

When using commercial transportation assets, on/offloading time parameters are restrictive. The length of allocated on/offloading time differs with the type of commercial asset used. General timelines addressed below are provided for commercial transportation/movement planning.

Buses

Buses are normally ordered to be in position for loading a minimum of 60 minutes before scheduled departure time. Units are responsible for ensuring buses depart in sufficient time to arrive at the final destination, and that they do not exceed the total time allocated for the movement. Buses are typically ordered by the hour.

Exceeding the contracted time will increase costs. Also, a delay in passenger movement could occur if the bus driver exceeds the maximum driving hours per day allowed by the US Department of Transportation and state transportation agencies.

Bonded Cargo

Normally, there is a 2-hour on/offloading time contracted for bonded cargo. Any delay that exceeds the contract will result in a user-delay charge. Delay charges vary by geographic location and company. Contact the local LMCC or TMO for current charges.

General Cargo

Typically, there is a 2-hour on/offloading time allowable under contracts for general cargo. Delay charges vary by geographic location and company. Contact the local LMCC or TMO for current charges.

Railcars

Normally, there is no specific time requirement to complete on/offloading of railcars. Units must finish loading in sufficient time to allow cars to be massed/staged to meet the scheduled "pull" time. The local TMO will provide units a "pull" time. Pull time is the train's actual departure time.

MHE

It is the using unit's responsibility to coordinate MHE and ensure operators are available during on/offloading of commercial assets. MHE requests are normally coordinated with the submission of unit TOT/TOP requests.

Cargo Staging

To expedite loading commercial assets, it is recommended that the unit's cargo and equipment be staged *at least 24 hours before* the desired pickup time.

Vehicle Loading Site

- Bonded cargo: staged at the loading site *not earlier than 6 hours before the desired pickup time but not later than 2 hours prior.*
- General cargo: staged *no later than 24 hours before the desired pickup time.*
- Vehicles/equipment: items should be staged at the loading site *no later than 24 hours before the desired pickup time.*

Railhead

Cargo and vehicles to be loaded on railcars should be staged at designated railhead staging areas *no later than 24 hours prior to desired loading time.* However, 36 hours prior is considered optimum to provide the rail inspectors ample time to conduct preloading inspections.

Documentation

Base and station TMOs may operate differently based on location. Some agencies require all commercial carriers to report to the local TMO to complete load documentation, while others opt to delegate the documentation process to the unit executing the move. Check local TMO SOP. If the documentation process is delegated to the moving unit, the following procedure is recommended:

Before any cargo, equipment or vehicle departs the base or station on commercial carriers, a completed government bill of landing (GBL) must be provided to the base or station TMO and deploying unit. The GBL forms the basis to determine the overall commercial transportation costs of the unit's deployment and provides chain-of-custody receipt accountability of unit equipment loaded by a carrier. It is the transaction receipt used to release funds to cover the transportation costs. Refer to the local TMO/LMCC procedures and DODR 4500.9-R, Part II for detailed information on the GBL.

HAZMAT Listing

All HAZMAT being shipped must be identified before requesting transportation. Figure 6-3 is a sample listing to be used and submitted with the commercial transportation request.

REQUEST TO SHIP HAZARDOUS MATERIALS
VIA COMMERCIAL TRANSPORTATION

EVERY COLUMN MUST BE COMPLETED AND TURNED IN TO THE MOVEMENT COORDINATOR WITH
THE TRANSPORTATION REQUEST. CALL xxx-xxxx FOR ASSISTANCE.

UNIT: _____

POC:_____

TELEPHONE NUMBER:_____

PKG or Item ID Number:_____

PROPER SHIPPING NAME Found in MCO 4030.19H	HAZARD CLASS OR DIVISION	UNITED NATIONS NUMBER	PACKING GROUP	QUANTITY/ WEIGHT	TOTAL QUANTITY/ WEIGHT

Figure 6-3. HAZMAT Listing for Commercial Transportation.

CHAPTER 7
SEALIFT

This chapter provides responsibilities, guidance, and procedures to plan and conduct sealift embarkation operations using US Navy (USN) amphibious shipping, Military Sealift Command shipping, and US or foreign flagged commercial shipping.

SECTION I
AMPHIBIOUS EMBARKATION PLANNING

Amphibious embarkation planning must begin early and proceed concurrently with all other planning; this cannot be overemphasized (JP 3.02.2). It requires detailed knowledge of the characteristics, capabilities, and limitations of ships and their relationship to the personnel, supplies, and equipment to be embarked. The timely and effective embarkation of units aboard ships can only be achieved through detailed planning and careful execution of plans. Amphibious embarkation planning requires constant coordination between all Marine and Navy command levels, and a mutual understanding of the requirements of each. Before an amphibious exercise or operation, unit embarkation personnel should completely review—

- JP 3.02.2.
- MCRP 4-11C, *Combat Cargo Operations Handbook.*
- Commander, Naval Surface Force, Atlantic Instruction (COMNAVSURFLANTINST) 3000.3, *Landing Force Spaces and Material Aboard COMNAVSURFLANT Ships.*
- Commander, Naval Surface Force Pacific, Instruction (COMNAVSURFPACINST) 4621.1A, *Standard Amphibious Embarkation Documentation Procedures.*
- COMNAVSURFPACINST 7320.1, *Troop Space Inventory/Inspection/Reimbursement Procedures.*

Note: The naval surface force instructions are being combined in a draft COMNAVSURFPACINST 4621.1B/ COMNAVSURFLANTINST 4621.1A/ MARFORLANTO 4620.2C/MARFORPACO 4621.1B, Landing Force Spaces, Ship's Loading Characteristics Pamphlet, and Amphibious Embarkation Documentation.

Landing Force Organization for Embarkation

The landing force (LF) can be organized for embarkation into embarkation groups, units, elements, and teams. For the purposes of this publication and ease of understanding, the LF organization for embarkation will be that of a MEU embarking as part of an expeditionary strike group (ESG).

Amphibious Embarkation Key Billets

To facilitate embarkation planning and execution, embarkation personnel should be familiar with the general duties and responsibilities of the key billets associated with an ESG/MEU deployment.

Commander, Landing Force

The commander, landing force (CLF) is the officer designated in the establishing directive or order initiating the amphibious operation to command the LF. The MEU commander, normally a colonel, is designated the CLF by billet. Embarkation planning responsibilities include—

- Determining LF requirements for assault shipping.
- Developing LF organization for embarkation.
- Identifying embarkation support requirements.
- Ensuring the preparation of detailed embarkation loading plans.

Commander, Amphibious Task Force

The commander, amphibious task force (CATF) is the USN officer designated in the establishing directive or order initiating the amphibious operation as commander of the amphibious task force (ATF). The amphibious squadron (PHIBRON) commander is designated the CATF by billet. Normally, the PHIBRON commander is a USN captain (billet title is commodore). Embarkation planning responsibilities include—

- Proposing assault shipping, landing craft, and sealift allocations to the commander, amphibious group.
- Providing ship's loading characteristics pamphlets (SLCPs) to the CLF.
- Organizing Navy forces (specifically CATF staff and Navy support element [NSE]) for embarkation.
- Preparing movement orders for ships.
- Approving LF embarkation and loading plans.
- Planning for external support (port operations).
- Advising the CLF on Navy support and naval forces embarkation requirements.

Ship's Commanding Officer

The ship's commanding officer (CO) is the highest authority aboard the ship. All personnel aboard ship, including embarked personnel, are subject to the CO's orders. All orders from the CO to embarked personnel will be transmitted through the commanding officer of troops (COT).

COT

On a ship that has embarked units, a designated officer (usually the senior embarking unit commander) is responsible for the administration, discipline, and training of all embarked units. The COT is ultimately responsible for the embarkation of LF personnel and assets aboard his respective ship.

LF Embarkation Officer

The MEU embarkation officer is the LF embarkation officer. His duties and responsibilities are—

- Heading the embarkation section on the special staff of the CLF.
- Preparing the LF embarkation plan for approval by the CLF.
- Coordinating all on/offloading LF activities.
- Maintaining a complete and current file of SLCPs for amphibious ships and loading characteristics data for other type ships that may be assigned to support the LF.
- Obtaining and maintaining the embarkation data for the LF.
- In conjunction with principal staff officers of the embarkation group and subordinate commanders, preparing the LF organization for embarkation and assignment to shipping (OE&AS).
- Obtaining data on materials handling requirements and MHE.
- Coordinating preparation of a berthing and loading schedule (BALS) with the ATF combat cargo officer (CCO).
- Advising team embarkation officers (TEOs) in the loading plans preparation.
- During the ship-to-shore movement, functioning as a member of the LF tactical-logistical (TACLOG) group on a designated ship.

- In concert with embarked units, the ATF CCO, appropriate staff officers, and department heads, coordinating the execution of the landing plan.
- Possessing knowledge in the use of LOGAIS, unit movement, and load planning systems.

ATF CCO

The ATF CCO is the PHIBRON Staff CCO for a MEU-sized LF. General duties and responsibilities are—

- Advising and assisting the CATF on all matters pertaining to the on/offloading of LF personnel, supplies, and equipment.
- Acting as liaison officer between the commodore and the corresponding embarking troop commander.
- Maintaining an SLCP file for those ships within the squadron.
- Reviewing all embarkation/debarkation plans.
- Maintaining copies of all load plans of ships in the ATF to include landing force operational reserve material (LFORM) stowage.
- Maintaining a complete and current file of LFORM loading plans for all ships assigned.
- In concert with the LF embarkation officer, appropriate staff officers and department heads, coordinating the execution of the landing plan.
- Coordinating staging and pre-embarkation inspections with the LF embarkation officer and preparing the BALS.
- Performing unit embarkation officer functions for the embarking NSE.
- Compiling and transmitting periodic reports to higher authority.
- Referring to MCRP 4-11C for a detailed list of ATF CCO duties.

TEO

The TEO is a commissioned officer assigned from the embarking unit forming the nucleus of the embarkation team. Assignment as a TEO is temporary but, upon appointment, the TEO should be provided formal TEO training and relieved of other duties. General TEO duties include—

- Acting as the direct representative of the embarkation team commander in matters pertaining to team embarkation and cargo loading.
- Maintaining liaison between the embarkation team commander and the ship's CO.
- Preparing detailed loading plans for the ship to which embarkation teams are assigned. The ship's CCO may assist the TEO in loading plans preparation.
- Coordinating and supervising loading plans execution.
- Assisting in planning for and executing offloading.
- Possessing knowledge in use of LOGAIS, unit movement, and load planning systems.

Ship's CCO

The ship's CCO is typically a commissioned limited duty or warrant officer qualified in the embarkation field. All amphibious assault ships are assigned a CCO with the exception of the dock landing ship (LSD) 41 Class where a Navy officer, normally the ship's first lieutenant (1stLT), functions as the ship's CCO. The CCO is a member of the ship's complement and functions as a special staff officer to the ship's CO. The amphibious assault ship-general purpose (LHA)/multipurpose (LHD) CCO is assigned three enlisted combat cargo assistants (CCAs). The amphibious transport dock (LPD)-17 CCO will have two CCAs, and the LPD-4 and dock landing ship (LSD)-49 class ship

CCOs have one CCA assigned. The CCA is a staff NCO and, like the CCO, is a member of the ship's complement. General duties of the CCO include—

- Acting as the direct representative of the ship's CO in embarkation matters and other LF-related issues.
- Maintaining liaison with the TEO and ATF CCO.
- Assisting the TEO in the preparation of detailed loading plans for the ship.
- In concert with the ATF and LF embarkation officers, appropriate staff officers and department heads, coordinating landing plan execution.
- Assisting in the planning and executing of embarkation/debarkation.
- Referring to MCRP 4-11C for a detailed list of the ship's CCO duties.

Transport Element Embarkation Officer

The transport element embarkation officer is usually a commissioned or warrant officer assigned the duties of the embarkation officer at the MSE level. Qualified assistants (MOS 0431) should be assigned early in the planning phase. The transport element embarkation officer may or may not be the unit embarkation officer while in garrison depending on the scope of the deployment and task organization. General duties are—

- Heading the embarkation section on the special staff of the MSE.
- Preparing, in conjunction with the principal subordinate commanders and staff officers of the element, the OE&AS table for approval by the MSE commander.
- Assigning and scheduling the use of cargo assembly areas, vehicle staging areas, and embarkation points to subordinate embarkation elements or teams. Assignments are based on marshalling area and embarkation area assignments made by the MEU embarkation officer.
- Preparing the complete unit embarkation plan for approval by the MSE commander.
- Providing required embarkation data to respective TEOs.
- Coordinating all MSE loading activities.
- During the ship-to-shore movement, functioning as a member of the TACLOG on a designated ship.

LF to USN Counterpart Relationships

See table 7-1.

Table 7-1. LF to USN Counterpart Relationships.

LF BILLET	USN BILLET	REMARKS
CLF	CATF	Coequal status. Together the forces of the CLF and CATF combined with USN surface and subsurface combatant ships comprise the ESG.
LF embarkation officer	CATF CCO	The LF embarkation officer and the CATF CCO conduct the predominance of the deliberate planning involved with the embarkation of the LF and NSE personnel, cargo, and equipment. The LF embarkation officer is the direct representative of the CLF in embarkation matters; likewise, the CATF CCO is the CATF's advisor on all LF on/offload matters.
COT	Ship's CO	The COT is designated the embarkation team commander. As such, the COT and ship's CO work together to ensure the personnel, cargo, and equipment assigned to their specific ship (team) is embarked IAW timelines. The COT reports to the CLF; the ship's CO reports to the CATF.
TEO	Ship's CCO	The detailed load planning and sequence of events relative to a specific ship are coordinated between the TEO and the ship's CCO. The TEO is the direct representative of the COT for embarkation matters; the ship's CCO represents the ship's captain as his embarkation expert.
Transport Element Embarkation Officer	N/A	The transport element embarkation officer does not have a USN counterpart. He is in general support of the TEOs. He will ensure that personnel, cargo, and equipment are marshalled, staged, moved, and embarked IAW published timelines. Element embarkation officers are found in all MSEs. They are the special staff officers in the area of embarkation within their MSEs. They receive guidance from the LF embarkation officer.

General Amphibious Ship Capabilities

For general amphibious ship capabilities and ship home stations, refer to MCRP 3-31B, *Amphibious Ships and Landing Craft Data Book*, and MCRP 4-11C. Figure 7-1 shows the first of the new LPD ship designs.

SLCP

Early in planning, embarkation personnel must review SLCPs for their assigned ships. The purpose of the SLCP is to provide embarking units information on the physical characteristics, methods of loading and stowage, operating procedures, and capabilities/limitations of a specific ship. Current SLCPs are available on each respective amphibious group's Web site. Each ship publishes an updated SLCP every 3 years or sooner if there is a major deviation from the published SLCP IAW COMNAVSURFLANTINST 9010.2/COMNAVSURFPACINST 9010.1, *Ship's Loading Characteristics Pamphlet (SLCP)*.

Embarked Troop Regulations

In addition to the SLCP, each amphibious assault ship has published embarked troop regulations (regs). Embark troop regs detail the policies and procedures that LF and NSE personnel must conform to while embarked. Embarkation personnel must completely review the SLCP and troop regs in the early stages of planning. Together, the SLCP and troop regs will provide important capabilities and constraints to be taken into consideration prior to detailed planning. General topics included in troop regs follow:

- Command relationships.
- Embarkation.
- Billeting, messing, medical, and sanitation.
- Emergency procedures and general regulations.
- Security.
- Cleaning and preservation.
- Discipline and confinement.
- Troop security force.
- Ammunition and HAZMAT handling.
- Debarkation.
- Communications.

LFORM

LFORM is a package of contingency and war reserve supplies prepositioned on amphibious ships. LFORM consists of rations, POL, field fortification material, and ammunition (Supply Classes I, III, IV, V[W], and V[A], respectively). The quantitative requirements for LFORM are based on notional planning figures for 15 days of sustainment for a MEU with 2,400 personnel. Figure 7-2 on page 7-6 shows the ten classes of supply.

Figure 7-1. LPD-17 *USS San Antonio*.

Class I		Rations	Food stuffs, subsistence, and rations.
Class II	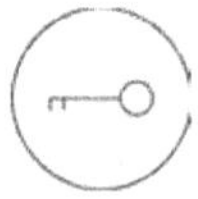	General Supply	Clothing, tentage, tool sets, individual equipment, and all textile or leather items.
Class III		POL	Petroleum products, including fuel, oil, and lubricants.
Class IV		Barrier Materials	Construction materials, barrier materials, lumber, pickets, barbed wire, concrete, bricks, and similar materials.
Class V		Ammunition	All ammunition and explosives including pyrotechnics and explosive training items.
Class VI		Personal Demand	Personal demand items, such as chewing gum, cigarettes, soft drinks, razor blades, candy, and other items that are selected by personal preference.
Class VII		Major End Items	Complete pieces of equipment by themselves that don't lose their identity through use, such as trucks, tanks, guns, and power units.
Class VIII	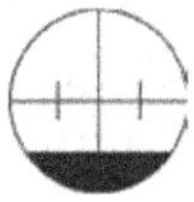	Medical	All medical supplies, such as medicines, medical equipment, and dressings.
Class IX		Repair Parts	Repair parts and subcomponents used as replacement parts for other equipment, including major subassemblies, such as engines and transmissions.
Class X		Civil Affairs Items	Items including equipment for economic development and general civilian assistance, such as farm tractors and school supplies.

Figure 7-2. Classes of Supply.

LFORM Supplement

Each LFORM-carrying amphibious ship's CCO or 1stLt is required to publish an LFORM supplement once all classes of LFORM have been embarked. The LFORM supplement is a load plan depicting stowage locations for all classes of LFORM. Prior to developing ship load plans, the ship's LFORM supplement must be reviewed.

Responsibility

It is the consolidated effort of the ship's staff to ensure LFORM is properly loaded and managed. The COT will also participate in the ship's periodic LFORM inspections. Inspections are not wall-to-wall inventories/inspections. The COT is inspecting the magazines and general cargo storage areas where LFORM products are stowed to assess the overall material condition of these contingency items. See COMNAVSURFLANTINST 4080.1/Commander Marine Forces Atlantic (COMMARFORLANT) Order 4000.10 series and COMNAVSURFPACINST 4080.1/Commander, Marine Forces Pacific (COMMARFORPAC) 4080.2 series for more information.

Issue

LFORM may only be issued or used in support of actual contingency operations or with the approval of a numbered fleet commander or COMMARFORLANT/COMMARFORPAC authority. Although the ship's CO, through his ordnance/weapons officer and supply officer, is ultimately responsible for LFORM onboard, the COT will ensure that LFORM ammunition and supplies are not inadvertently mixed with training allocations.

Embarkation Milestones

Early in the planning phase, the LF embarkation officer and ATF CCO will coordinate to develop embarkation milestones to be included in the ESG/MEU plan of action and milestones message sent to all the units of the amphibious force. Embarkation milestones identify actions and reports required to effect planning and embarkation of all LF and NSE assets throughout the ESG/MEU predeployment work-up period through the final deployment load-out. The following reports are critical to this effort:

- NSE augmentation message.
- Landing craft availability table (LCAT).
- BALS.
- Valid surface landing plan/serial assignment table and the helicopter team wave and serial assignment table.
- Ship load plans and LFORM supplement.
- Shipboard LF accommodations inspection or shipboard inspection summary reports.
- LFORM shortfall/ammunition shortfall message.
- Embarked personnel and material report (EPMR).
- LFORM inspection report.
- SLCP validation report.

See MCRP 4-11C for detailed information on reports listed above. Also see appendix J for a detailed listing of milestones as related to the designated embarkation day (E-day).

UDL

Using MDSS II, all embarking units (to include the LF, CATF staff, and NSE) will provide a UDL identifying all vehicles, equipment, boxes, pallets, and containers to the designated TEO for consolidation. The TEO will merge the UDLs, complete carrier assignments in the embarkation workbench module, generate TCNs, and then export the resulting embarkation plan file to ICODES to develop detailed load plans. Embarkation personnel at the unit level may have to provide UDL development and load planning support for up to three TEOs.

Load Planning

The TEO is responsible for his assigned ship's ICODES ship load plan deck diagrams. The load plan will incorporate all cargo, vehicles, and equipment authorized to be loaded in LF ("green") stowage spaces on the assigned ship. The load plan will include LFORM and the ship's organic equipment; i.e., MHE, or aviation support equipment from a UDL provided by each ship's CCO. Load plan development is a team effort of the TEO and his assigned team embarkation assistants, the ship's CCO/1stLT, the LF embarkation officer, and the ATF CCO. The load plan is designed to support the LF landing plan/ scheme of maneuver ashore. All ship load planning will be accomplished using the data resident in the unit's UDL.

Supporting Documents

When submitting the ICODES deck diagrams to the COT for review and approval, the TEO will ensure that the following documents are included. Refer to JP 3.02.2, for additional information.

- Load plan cover sheet.
- Cargo and loading analysis table.
- Vehicle summary and priority table.
- UP&TT summary report.

Load Plan Approval

The TEO, in conjunction with the LF embarkation officer, develops the load plan and submits it to the COT for review/approval. Once the load plan has been approved by the COT, it is normally submitted to the LF embarkation officer, then to the ship's CO via the CCO. The CCO will verify that all requirements and any restrictions are considered in the load plan. The CCO typically staffs the load plan through the chief engineer, damage control assistant, and the ship's 1st LT prior to submitting it to the ship's CO. Once approved by the ship's CO, deviations from the load plan are not authorized without the express consent from the COT and the ship's CO.

Templates

Load planners must ensure each loaded item's template contains the following minimum information:
- Vehicles:
  - Vehicle priority number.
  - Landing serial number.
  - Vehicle height.
  - Marriage designator (if required).
  - Vehicle description.
  - Owning organization (UIC).
  - Vehicle weight.
  - TCN.
- Containers/pallets:
  - UIC.
  - Description of contents.
  - Gross weight.
  - Height.
  - Offload priority number.
  - TCN.

Types of Loading

Administrative

An administrative loading method gives primary consideration to achieving maximum use of billeting and cargo space.

Combat

A combat loading method gives primary consideration to providing the ability to debark troops and cargo ready for combat rather than for economy of space. Combat loading has three categories:

- Combat unit loading.
- Combat organizational loading.
- Combat spread loading.

JP 3-02.2 provides additional information on types of loading.

Note: For amphibious embarkation planning, all loads will be combat loads.

Broken Stowage

In stowing cargo, a percentage of space is invariably lost between boxes, vehicles, and around stanchions/obstructions. For planning purposes, these losses are expressed in terms of a percentage known as broken stowage. JP 3.02.2 provides detailed information on broken stowage factors and broken stowage loss.

Appendix K, Sample Embarkation Plan

Embarkation guidance relative to a sealift deployment will be provided via a published embarkation plan or embarkation LOI. The LF will publish the overall embarkation plan and submit it to the MSEs and the CATF. MSEs will subsequently publish an embarkation LOI for their subordinate units. See appendix K.

External Support Requirements

The LF embarkation officer will coordinate with the LF operations (G-3/S-3) and logistics (G-4/S-4) sections to satisfy requirements that affect the entire MAGTF; e.g., port and beach requests, ship berthing/loading scheduling, portable toilets or commercial transportation. The TEO or element/unit embarkation officer will identify any specific external requirements to the LF embarkation officer. Final coordination of support requirements leads to the movement, marshalling and staging plans, which are used by LF and CATF planners to develop a BALS. Once completed, the CATF will publish a BALS naval message to all ATF units and, approximately 10 days prior to E-day, the LF, LMCC, MSEs, and supporting port authority representatives will

join for a port-opening meeting that addresses the following concerns.

Transportation

Transportation requests in excess of organic assets will be forwarded to the LF movement coordinator. The movement coordinator, usually the MEU S-4 chief, will be identified early in planning. The movement coordinator will include all MSE requirements and attend all LMCC TOT/TOP movement conferences necessary to finalize the movement plan.

MHE

Nonorganic MHE support will be requested by the element embarkation officer in conjunction with movement requirements and submitted to the LF movement coordinator. Request for support will include lighting, washdown points, forklifts, cranes and/or wreckers to support the movement plan.

Slings and Cargo Net

Devices used to lift heavy objects include slings for vehicles, chime hooks, pallets, bridles and cargo nets. Coordination with the TEO is required to ensure the ship has the appropriate equipment. If equipment requires special slings or other lifting devices not organic to the ship, the embarking unit must provide them.

Dunnage, Shoring, Chocking or Blocking and Bracing Materials

It is the using unit's responsibility to ensure it has enough of these materials to secure loads, protect unit equipment, and adhere to ship regulations. A review of the SLCP or liaison with the ship will indicate existing requirements.

If dunnage, shoring, chocking or blocking and bracing materials are required that are beyond the using unit's capabilities, embarking units will prepare consolidated estimates and submit them to the LF embarkation officer. The LF embarkation officer will coordinate with the S-4, supply section to source the requirement.

The SLCPs, JP 3-02.2, and MCRP 4-11C contain additional information on these items.

Troop Embarkation

Troops embark amphibious assault ships by helicopter, landing craft, ship's accommodation ladder, and roll-on/roll-off (RO/RO) ramps. The safest and most efficient means will be determined through careful coordination between the LF embarkation officer and the ATF and ship's CCO per embarkation plans. Refer to MCRP 4-11C and the SLCP for detailed procedures. Two major phases of troop embarkation are advance party and main body.

Advance Party

The advance party is routinely embarked 24 to 48 hours before the main body at the SPOE. Detailed information on personnel augmentation requirements is included in the SLCP. The advance party consists of—

- The ship's platoon.
- Cooks.
- Food service attendants (with current mess physicals).
- Guard personnel (if required by ship).
- Billeting guides.
- Any other ship augmentees.

Main Body

The main body movement from the garrison location to the SPOE should be phased to prevent congestion upon arrival at the pier. Upon arrival at the SPOE, the main body will form into loading teams or sticks by berthing area. Billeting guides will meet loading teams at the pier and escort them into their respective berthing areas. Billeting guides should be made available to provide squad-size or platoon-size unit tours for the first few days to ensure Marines are familiar with all spaces aboard ship.

LF Spaces

Serviceable LF spaces are key to the overall combat readiness of an amphibious ship. Working with the ship's department heads, the CCO aboard each ship ensures all LF spaces are available for troop embarkation within 48 hours of notice. Before troops embark, a joint inspection (JI) of all spaces must be conducted by ship and LF billeting representatives. A billeting officer should be designated for each amphibious ship. Refer to MCRP 4-11C, COMNAVSURFLANTINST 3000.3, COMNAVSURFPACINST 7320.1 or COMNAVSURFPACINST 4621.1A.

Inspection of Troop Living Spaces

Prior to embarkation and debarkation, a habitability inspection between the COT and ship's representatives will be conducted in all LF berthing, administrative, and personal hygiene spaces. This inventory/inspection will identify the total quantity and condition of furnishings and the quality of life condition of all LF spaces. The COT is responsible for ensuring the habitability inventory/inspection is properly and promptly conducted.

Reimbursement for Inventory Losses

Upon completion of the debarkation inventory/inspection, the ship's representative will submit an initial report of missing or damaged property to the COT for reconciliation and reimbursement of associated costs. Unreconciled items or costs will be forwarded concurrently for resolution via the unit's chain of command to COMMARFORLANT/COMMARFORPAC and COMMNAVSURFLANT/COMNAVSURFPAC via the ship's chain of command.

Encroachment

Encroachment exists when ship's company uses LF spaces without authorization. Two situations when ship's company may be authorized to occupy LF spaces are—

- 48-hour restoration: the ship is able to restore the spaces to their original purpose within 48 hours.
- Permanent authorization: ship's company can permanently occupy LF spaces with an approved ship alteration.

Troop Bedding

Amphibious ship COs are required to provide—

- One mattress.
- Four sheets.
- One or two blankets (one blanket for COMNAVSURFLANT ships; two blankets for COMNAVSURFPAC ships).
- One pillow.
- Two pillowcases.

SECTION II
MILITARY SEALIFT COMMAND

The mission of the Military Sealift Command is to provide an immediate sealift capability in support of a contingency operation, armed conflict or other emergency.

Measurement Units

Knowledge of the weight and volume measurements below is required to plan for Military Sealift Command ship loads:

- Long ton: 2,240 pounds.
- Short ton: 2,000 pounds.
- Metric ton: 2,200 pounds.
- Measurement ton: 40 cubic feet.
- Bale cubic capacity: the space available for loading cargo up to the inside of the cargo

battens on the frames and to the underside of the beams that make up the superstructure of a ship. This measurement in cubic feet is used to compute the space available for general cargo.

Military Sealift Command SLCPs

Military Sealift Command SLCPs are similar to those prepared for amphibious ships. Unit embarkation personnel should contact their HHQ to obtain a specific SLCP. For general information on loading characteristics and considerations, refer to Military Traffic Management Command Transportation Engineering Agency (MTMCTEA) Pamphlet (PAM) 700-4, *Vessel Characteristics for Ship Loading*.

Loading Military Sealift Command Ships

The SDDC, formerly MTMC, is the agency responsible for the in-port cargo handling and ship loading for Military Sealift Command ships. Embarkation planners must—

- Make liaison with SDDC early in planning to identify ship loading and Military Sealift Command ship load planning capabilities and constraints.
- Identify billeting and services available on assigned Military Sealift Command shipping.
- Coordinate with the ship's master or 1st mate on the number of embarked personnel. Because of limited facilities and messing and berthing capacity, most Military Sealift Command ships are restricted to the number of personnel that can accompany the embarked vehicles and equipment load.

- Determine if cots; sleeping bags; meals, ready to eat (MREs); water; and heads are needed.
- Prepare and submit Worldwide Port System export files from MDSS II and ship load plans to the SDDC.
- Identify onload support requirements to the LF embarkation office. The LF embarkation office will arrange for stevedores and longshoremen for loading and securing loads.

Unloading Military Sealift Command Ships

SDDC is also the agency responsible for the unloading of Military Sealift Command ships at the SPOD. Embarkation planners should coordinate offload requirements with HHQ and/or SDDC.

SECTION III
MARITIME PREPOSITIONING FORCE

Background

MPF remains one of the Marine Corps' premier deployment options available to support our expeditionary maneuver warfare concepts. Coupled with strategic airlift, use of MPF greatly reduces the deployment timeline by having equipment pre-staged aboard maritime prepositioning ships (MPS).

MPSRONS

Sixteen MPS are specially configured and assigned to MPS squadrons (MPSRONs) to transport nearly everything a Marine needs for initial military operations—from tanks and ammunition, to food, fuel, spare parts, and engine oil. The ships were built or modified beginning in the mid-1980s and are on location

in the western Pacific Ocean, the Indian Ocean, and the Mediterranean Sea.

The MPF is organized into three MPSRONs, each commanded by a Navy captain. MPSRON ONE, usually located in the Atlantic Ocean or Mediterranean Sea, has five ships. MPSRON TWO, usually located at Diego Garcia, has five ships. See figure 7-3 for an example. MPSRON THREE, normally in the Guam/Saipan area, has six ships. In addition to Marine Corps-designated ships, MPSRON staffs also oversee all other prepositioning ships in their geographic operating areas.

MPSRON ONE

- MV PFC William B. Baugh.
- MV 2nd LT John P. Bobo.
- SS PFC Eugene A. Obregon.
- USNS LCpl Roy M. Wheat.
- MV PFC Dewayne T. Williams.

Figure 7-3. MV 1ˢᵗ LT Baldomero Lopez (T-AK 3010) Container and RO/RO Ship.

MPSRON TWO

- MV Sgt William R. Button.
- MV SS SGT Matej Kocak.
- MV 1stLt Baldomero Lopez.
- MV Pvt Franklin J. Phillips.
- USNS GySgt Fred W. Stockham.

MPSRON THREE

- MV PFC James Anderson, Jr.
- MV 1ˢᵗLT Alex Bonnyman.
- MV Cpl Louis J. Hauge, Jr.
- MV 1ˢᵗLT Jack Lummus.
- USNS 1ˢᵗLT Harry L. Martin.
- SS Maj Stephen W. Pless.

Each MPSRON carries sufficient equipment and supplies to sustain approximately 15,000 personnel, (a Marine expeditionary brigade), for up to 30 days. Each ship can discharge cargo pierside or while anchored offshore using lighterage carried aboard. This capability gives the Marine Corps the ability to operate in developed and underdeveloped areas of the world. For more information on MPF operations, refer to MCWP 3-32, *Maritime Prepositioning Force Operations*. Detailed information on MPF and each MPS prepositioned load can be found on the Blount Island Command's Marine Corps Prepositioning Information Center Web site at http://www.mcpic.matcombic.usmc.mil/about MCPIC.htm.

SECTION IV
JOINT HIGH SPEED VESSEL

Background

The joint high speed vessel (JHSV) is a concept-based experimental craft used to help refine naval expeditionary concepts and develop capabilities for future joint force commanders. Key capabilities are its speed and cargo- and vehicle-carrying capacity. Within 16 hours it can carry notional loads of up to 290 personnel, approximately 25 vehicles, and limited rotary-wing aircraft, and deliver it 600 miles from its origin.

Western Pacific Express

The Western Pacific (WESTPAC) Express is a modified high speed vessel (HSV) designed to support the movement of III MEF forces from Okinawa and MCAS, Iwakuni, Japan to locations throughout the WESTPAC region. It provides the commander the flexibility of an intratheater lift capability. The WESTPAC Express was the foundation for launching the JHSV concept and serves as a test bed for future HSV projects. See figure 7-4 and appendix L.

Figure 7-4. WESTPAC Express.

CHAPTER 8
AIRLIFT

This chapter provides guidance for units planning and preparing the air movement of personnel, supplies, and equipment by AMC-provided aircraft (fig. 8-1), operational support airlift (OSA) aircraft, and common-user, commercial or organic aircraft. These airlift resources support JCS-directed deployments/exercises, unit deployment program unit rotations or unit training deployments.

Figure 8-1. C-17 Globemaster III.

Planning Requirements

Air movement planning must be flexible to facilitate rapid changes to the number and type of aircraft provided, the allowable cabin loads of assigned aircraft, and mission requirements. Basic information, detailed data, and knowledge of planning and preparations procedures are required to accurately register a unit's airlift requirements via airlift requests to HHQs for scheduled exercise planning or real-world contingencies. DODR 4500.9-R, Part III lists basic AMC aircraft capabilities and loading considerations.

Basic Information

Embarkation personnel involved in airlift planning and operations at all levels must be familiar with—

- Capabilities of the departure and arrival airfields to support the number and type of aircraft to be used.
- Airfield operating hours and their effects on the movement.
- Availability of support equipment at the departure and arrival airfields and staging and marshalling areas.
- POCs at each location supporting the airlift.
- Availability of permanent or expeditionary messing and billeting facilities.
- Any unique requirements inherent to the unit.

Detailed Data

It is important that timely, accurate data be developed, validated, and provided to HHQs that forecasts the quantities of personnel, supplies, and types of equipment to be airlifted. Unit planning will be continuous and supported by use of the MDSS II and AALPS.

Knowledge

Unit personnel must be trained to identify, prepare, and marshal their cargo and equipment for air movement operations. T/E-specific items that have airlift-unique characteristics or special loading requirements should be documented in unit desktop procedures and turnover folders. Cargo and equipment configurations and/or characteristics that require special planning/handling for airlift include (but are not limited to) the following:

- Any item requiring palletizing that exceeds a length of 20 feet.
- Items that exceed a height of 96 inches.

- Vehicles having an axle load in excess of 10,000 pounds or a wheel load exceeding 5,000 pounds.
- All hazardous cargo.

Qualifications

Skills of personnel assigned to plan and supervise air movement operations should be continuously reviewed and evaluated.

United States Air Force Training

Contact the MSC embarkation office to coordinate United States Air Force (USAF) MTTs or take advantage of scheduled USAF sponsored training. See chapter 2 for courses.

Unit Training

Organizations should conduct indoctrination and periods of instruction and/or MOT for air movement operations. Such training should include, (but not be limited to) the following:

- Waterproofing of cargo/equipment, tactical markings, banding and palletizing.
- Building, weighing, and marking 463L pallets.
- Reduction of vehicles and equipment heights, and cargo mobile loading techniques.
- Weighing, marking, and center of balance computation techniques for cargo, vehicles, and equipment.
- Hazardous cargo familiarization and preparation.
- Airlift documentation requirements.
- Plane team commanders' (PTCs') responsibilities.

Special Assignment Airlift Mission Requests

Special assignment airlift missions (SAAMs) are airlift requirements, including JCS-directed/coordinated exercise requirements that require special consideration due to the number of PAX involved, weight or size of cargo, urgency of movement, sensitivity or other factors that preclude the use of channel airlift.

All SAAM requests from the MSC will be submitted in the format in DODR 4500.9-R, Part I and Part II. Submission dates and message formats will be per local SOP. SAAM requests are—

- Routinely prepared and submitted when requesting AMC airlift in support of unit deployment program unit rotations and training deployments (continental United States [CONUS] and/or outside the CONUS) when the use of JOPES has not been directed.
- Initiated and *verified* for accuracy by the deploying unit, the MSC embarkation officer, the MEF SMO, and *validated* by the MARFOR SMO.
- Forwarded to USTRANSCOM by the MARFOR SMO to AMC for sourcing of the aircraft.
- Typically required to be submitted to the MSC accompanied by an electronic copy of the notional load plan for each plane load requested.

Joint Airborne/Air Transportability Training and Dual-Role Airlift Support Requests

The use of joint airborne/air transportability training (JA/ATT) and dual-role (DR) airlift support provides an opportunity to conduct joint USMC and USAF aircrew qualifications and load team proficiency skills development. Through the use of JA/ATT missions and DR, aviation elements are provided with strategic airlift assets at no cost in support of scheduled events (training, exercise, and employment plans). DRs are used to take advantage of aerial refueling missions to move cargo and equipment with the refueling mission. When using a JA/ATT, the supported unit is responsible for MHE support at the APOE and APOD. Transportation of required MHE support needs to be considered during the airlift budgeting process. JA/ATT missions include—

- Air drop.
- Air assault.

- Static load.
- Certification of new equipment.
- Combat support training (flare, leaflet, spray).

JA/ATT airlift is **not** point-to-point transportation. JA/ATT requests are typically submitted at the monthly CONUS JA/ATT conference or quarterly WESTPAC JA/ATT conference using a JA/ATT worksheet. JA/ATT mission scheduling usually occurs six times per year at every other monthly conference. DRs are scheduled via the Internet using Web-based applications. More information can be obtained from HHQ G-3, embarkation or strategic mobility office on local JA/ATT procedures.

Note: DRs are used to take advantage of re-fueling air missions to move cargo and equipment with the refueling mission. If a DR associated with a pre-existing Marine air refueling mission falls out (is not re-quired, is cancelled or cannot be filled), the secondary requirement/request of the DR (typically cargo/PAX movement) will also fall out.

Additional JA/ATT and DR procedures can be obtained through the respective chain of command S-3/G-3 and/or S-4/G-4 offices.

Commercial Air Movement Requests

Commercial air movement (CAM) requests are routinely prepared and submitted when requesting commercial chartered or scheduled passenger airlift in support of unit movements within CONUS and when the use of JOPES has not been directed. All CAM requests shall be submitted IAW local SOP. CAM requests shall include the deployment and redeploy-ment requirements.

Cost Estimates

US Government airlift rates and non-US Govern-ment airlift rates publications contain airlift and transportation working capital fund (TWCF) air-lift rates directed by pertinent regulations and Office of the Secretary of Defense guidance. All rates are identified in the four publications listed below. The information in these publications, coupled with airfield information from the Air Force Regulation (AFR) 76-11, *US Government Rate Tariffs*, are used to determine SAAM and channel airlift costs:

- *US Government, DOD Airlift Rates.*
- *US Government, Non-DOD Airlift Rates*; e.g., Department of State uses these rates.
- *Non-US Government/Foreign Military Sales Rates*; e.g., foreign governments use these rates.
- *Charters-Special Assignment Airlift Missions (SAAMs), Joint Chiefs of Staff Exercises (JCSE), and Contingencies for the Transporta-tion Working Capital Fund (TWCF), and Non-TWCF Aircraft.*

Airfield and mission timing (aircraft flight times) information can be obtained as follows:

- The joint flow and analysis system for trans-portation (JFAST) on the Internet provides a look-up function to identify ICAO codes for airfields and an air distance calculator that will generate the flight time from the selected APOE and APOD and any interim stops. The JFAST calculator can be found at http://www.jfast.org/Tools/Port2PortAirDist/default.asp.
- AFR 76-11 provides an index of station identi-fiers/air terminal identification codes. The AMC's Airfield Suitability and Restrictions Report and IATA also provide listings of ICAO codes to determine airlift rates. Any fur-ther assistance on codes can be obtained from the HHQs embarkation office, affiliated TALCE or any military airfield.
- Airlift rate information, ICAO codes, and other airlift planning tools can be accessed on AMC-provided Web site at https://tacc.scott.af.mil.

- The sample worksheet below provides a "fill-in-the-blank" format to compute the SAAM cost for a Marine unit using one C-141 flying one mission (sortie) from Cherry Point, NC, to Roosevelt Roads, Puerto Rico.

BASING POINT: CHARLESTON AFB, SC	
Charleston AFB, SC (KCHS) to MCAS Cherry Pt, NC (KNKT)	0 hr 26 min Flying Hrs (Position)
MCAS Cherry Pt, NC (KNKT) to NAS Roosevelt Roads (TJNR)	3 hr 04 min Flying Hrs (Sortie)
NAS Roosevelt Roads (TJNR) to Charleston AFB, SC (KCHS)	3 hr 06 min Flying Hrs (Deposition)
Total Flying Hours	6 hr 36 min Flying Hrs
C-141 Hourly Rate (Table 1 DOD User)	$5,489.00
Flying Hours x C-141 rate	6.60
Mission Cost	**$36,227.40**

After an initial estimate is completed, consider the following to reduce the overall cost of the SAAM:

- Request *one aircraft vice two* where possible to reduce positioning/depositioning costs.
- Request a *larger movement window* to reduce the number of aircraft required to operate the mission.
- Plan *dove-tails*: using one aircraft to support deploying/redeploying units from the same APOD/APOE by coordinating the modification of the aircraft internal load configuration and unit arrival, staging, and departure times.
- Submit *horse-blanket requests* to use a previously scheduled tanker; i.e., KC-10/KC-135, to carry PAX/cargo while executing the refueling mission. Horse-blanket requests are primarily used for, but not limited to, MAW units.

Airlift and Transportation Working Capitol Fund

The TWCF is a management tool used by AMC to allocate DOD airlift and provide flexibility to expand to meet changing airlift needs. This management system provides visibility of costs for the air movement of PAX and cargo. Additional TWCF information can be accessed via AMC/tanker airlift control center (TACC) Internet Web sites.

Airlift Forecasts

Local procedures dictate requirements for forecasting airlift needs, typically short (quarterly) or long (yearly) range forecasts that depict all scheduled, coordinated, and/or pending airlift requirements. The MSC embark section normally consolidates subordinate unit SAAM requirements and submits them to the MEF SMO who, in turn, consolidates and forwards the entire MEF forecast to the MARFOR SMO. Accurate forecasting of airlift requirements will help to ensure appropriate airlift funding and assets will be provided in the amounts, quantities, and configurations needed or desired. Changes to the *short range* forecast are required when there are any additions, deletions, and/or significant changes to the PAX/cargo load configurations that would affect airlift requirements.

OSA Requests

OSA requests are routinely prepared and submitted when requesting Joint Operational Support Airlift Command and Navy Air Logistics Office (NALO) airlift in support of unit and/or administrative movements. All OSA requests will be prepared IAW DODR 4500.9-R, Part I using DD Form 2768, *Military Air Passenger/Cargo Request,* with further guidance in MCO 4631.10A, *Operational Support Airlift Management.*

JOPES Airlift Requests

Normally, airlift in support of an OPLAN is provided via a designated TPFDD plan ID number within the JOPES. See chapter 5 and appendix A for more information.

Changes to Airlift Requests

Changes to requests are required when the desired movement dates require change and/or the cargo/PAX detail may impact the quantity/type airlift support requirements. Local SOP will dictate requirements for identifying changes.

AMC Channel Movement

Channel airlift is a common user airlift service provided on a scheduled basis between two points. These requests will be submitted IAW DODR 4500.9-R, Part I, Part II, and local SOP. The two types of channel airlift service, requirements and frequency, and examples of how the Marine Corps uses them follow.

Requirements Airlift Channel

Service is provided based on the amount of cargo to move through a given established channel.

> **Example**
>
> When 20 tons of cargo is staged awaiting airlift for an established requirements channel destination, the channel mission is operated.

Frequency Airlift Channel

Service is flown on a scheduled basis.

> **Example**
>
> Every Tuesday and Thursday an AMC channel mission is operated to Diego Garcia in the Indian Ocean for US forces (to include MPSRON TWO). This AMC frequency channel was established to satisfy an ongoing resupply requirement for the Navy. The frequency channel validator (Chief of Naval Operations in this case) must continue to guarantee AMC enough revenue to pay for the frequency service/keep the channel operating.

Uses for Channel Airlift

The USMC uses AMC channel airlift to move individuals or small groups of personnel, high priority cargo (normally supply/resupply items) and unaccompanied baggage (code J shipment). Passenger and cargo/mail channel rates are used by the TMO to determine airlift channel traffic.

> **Example**
>
> Marines and dependents who fly to Okinawa on a Northwest Airlines B747 from Los Angeles are flying on a contracted AMC channel aircraft.

Air Clearance Authority

Each branch of the Military Services has an airlift clearance authority (ACA) that reviews and electronically clears (approves) channel movement requirements. The Marine Corps' ACA is located at Marine Corps Logistics Base, Barstow. During peacetime most Marine Corps cargo sent via AMC airlift channel is destined for Hawaii or Okinawa and Iwakuni, Japan. Cargo and personnel for the forward-deployed MEUs from both coasts are sent via AMC airlift channel as well. The ACA also clears airlift channel cargo during wartime.

Multimode – SAAM Comparison

Channel airlift is used to move small amounts of PAX and cargo, typically at a cost less than that of a SAAM. However, APOEs and APODs where channel missions are operated are limited in number/location. Cargo may not be able to move at the desired time. On the other hand, SAAM airlift is used to move entire units (costs more than the channel). The requesting unit can request specific APOEs/APODs and desired/required movement dates.

Real World Cost Comparison Example

A radio battalion (RadBn) detachment (DET) needs to move from Hawaii to Korea in January. The amounts used in the example below for sealift and airlift are based on fiscal year 2004 rates and subject to change. The DET consists of 20 PAX; eight HMMWVs; four QUADCONs; and 1,000 pounds of security cargo requiring two escorts.

Note: If these items are transported via Military Sealift Command shipping, they may have to be containerized, a hidden cost to be added to the port-handling and inland transportation costs associated with the sealift.

This lift requirement equates to two C-141 equivalent loads. Often, a SAAM request would be submitted for two C-141's to support this deployment. For purposes of this comparison, the notional costs to move the DET via mixed, common-user transportation modes are—

COMMON-USER COSTS	
18 PAX @ $858 each (Via commercial airlines or AMC channel)	$15,444
8 HMMWVs and 4 QUADCONs (Via SDDC Liner Ocean Transportation Program)	$11,523
Security cargo/2 escorts (Via AMC channel airlift)	$4,180*
Total	$31,147
* Rates based on FY04 TWCF rates of 246.4 cents per pound for 1,000 pounds of cargo ($2,464) from Hickam AFB, Hawaii to Osan AB Korea, plus $858 x 2 for the 2 escorts ($1,716).	
SAAM COSTS	
C-141 Costs	$329,340
MCAS Miramar (KNKX) to Hickam AFB, HI (PHIK) to Osan AB, Korea (RKSO) to MCAS Miramar (KNKX)	
Savings: $298,193	

Considerations

Multimode shipments require more lead-time for coordination. The sealift leg of this shipment could take 2 to 3 weeks or 8 to10 weeks, depending on ship availability and staging times. The key question to answer is is the cost savings worth the additional time? In this case the unit cannot likely do without the equipment for 8 to 10 weeks (valuable training work-up time), a factor that needs to be weighed. Cost is not necessarily the key determinate in selecting modes of transportation.

Airlift Documentation

As identified in DODR 4500.9-R, Part I and Part III the following forms are used for load planning and documenting cargo and PAX to be airlifted. Airlift documentation is a deploying unit's responsibility.

Aircraft Load Plans

All organizations will prepare and submit aircraft load plans using the MDSS II UDL and AALPS. Typically, a minimum of seven copies of the final load plan are required for movement. Refer to DODR 4500.9-R, Part III, Appendix O for documentation requirements.

One copy of the final load plan should be submitted to the MSC AC/S, G-4 embarkation office upon completion of the moving unit/USAF JI typically not later than 24 hours before the scheduled aircraft departure. Refer to local SOP for submission requirements. When it is not feasible to use an automated load planning system, units will prepare and submit manual load plans using the appropriate DD Form 2130 series forms, *Aircraft Load Plans*. When the use of JOPES load plans is directed, the unit must be prepared to submit C-17 and C-5 aircraft load plan options to AMC/TACC, prior to a mission being assigned.

Passenger Manifests

Accurate passenger manifests are mandatory to ensure accountability of personnel embarking aboard aircraft. Responsibility for the preparation, correction, and validation of the passenger manifest rests with the G-1/S-1. Assignment of a G-1/S-1 representative to the deploying unit's ALE for passenger manifesting and reporting purposes during movement operations is required. All passenger manifests will be prepared and attached to each submitted aircraft load plan in the format and quantities listed in DODR 4500.9-R, Part III, Appendix AD.

Duties and Responsibilities of the Plane Team Commander

Refer to DODR 4500.9-R, Part III for detailed information on the PTC duties and responsibilities. Copies of this information should be provided with the passenger manifests to each PTC assigned.

Cargo and Equipment Preparations

Preparing supplies and equipment for air shipment is a unit responsibility and will normally be accomplished in the unit marshalling areas. Preparation includes packing, crating, unitizing, and marking supplies and equipment, and preparing vehicles for loading (including provision of special slings if required).

Computing Center of Balance

DODR 4500.9-R, Part III, Appendix F provides detailed information on the proper procedures for computing the center of balance of the various types of equipment and vehicles.

463L Pallet System

This is the cargo palletizing system used by the DTS for air movement. For detailed pallet building instructions, refer to DODR 4500.9-R, Part III.

See figure 8-2 on page 8-8. The 463L system consists of a 463L pallet, two side nets, and one top net. This system is a worldwide mobility asset and is controlled and monitored by USTRANSCOM via AMC IAW DODR 4500.9-R, *Part VI, Management and Control of Intermodal Containers and System 463-L Equipment.*

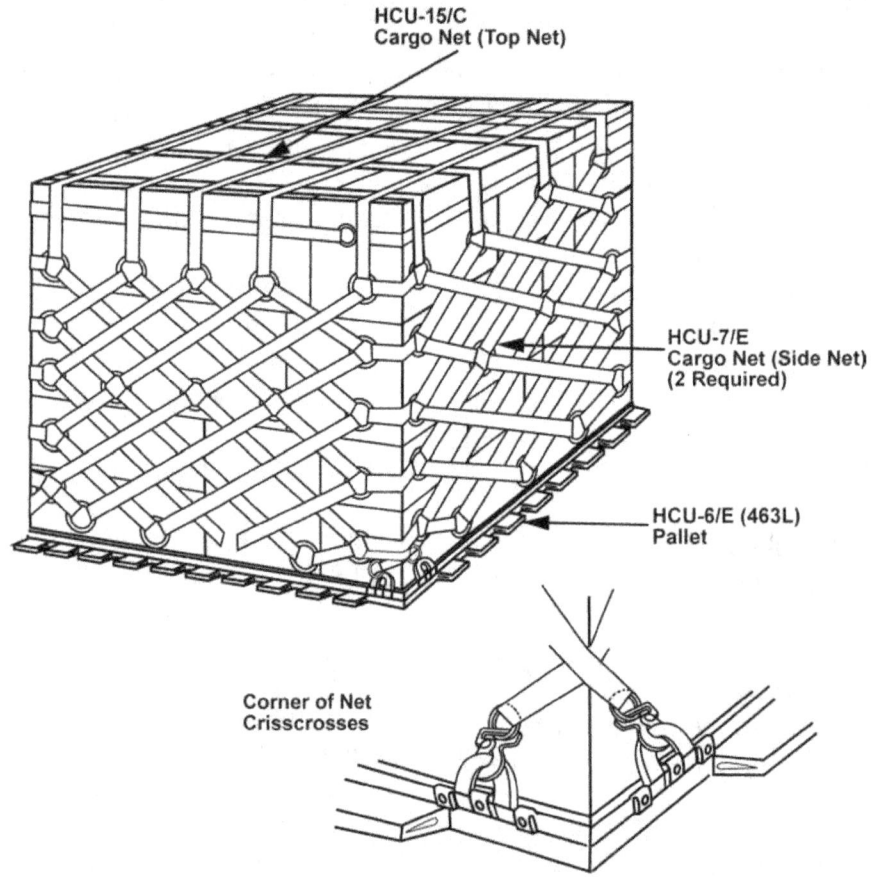

Figure 8-2. 463L Pallet System.

Shoring and Dunnage

Shoring and dunnage is required when tracked vehicles, helicopters, metal containers, bins, and vehicles with hard rubber tires are loaded. Shoring and dunnage prevents damage to the aircraft cargo floor and 463L pallets. Providing shoring and dunnage is the responsibility of the moving unit. Requirements should be identified prior to or early in deployment planning. Units should maintain 50 percent of the total required shoring and dunnage for air and amphibious embarkation. Shoring and dunnage will be stored in the unit area and, to the maximum extent possible, properly preserved and protected from the elements. Information about the sizes and quantities of lumber for the required dunnage should always be available so units can procure additional shoring or dunnage in a timely manner should the need occur; i.e., open purchase requisition.

Marshalling and Staging

This is the deploying unit's area of responsibility. The marshalling area is located at home station or the APOE in certain situations. If a unit desires the marshalling area to be located at the APOE, coordination with the DACG and/or TALCE must be made prior to the first chalk's arrival. The unit prepares equipment/supplies, assembles them into chalks (load order) for shipment, and delivers them to the alert holding area where administrative control is turned over to the DACG.

It is the deploying unit's responsibility to arrange for the movement of their equipment to and from the designated marshalling and staging areas. The using unit is responsible to ensure sufficient MHE is available at the APOE/APOD.

Movement of Individual Weapons and Small Arms Ammunition Aboard Commercial Aircraft

DODR 4500.9-R, Part I and Part III provide detailed information on moving individual weapons on contracted commercial aircraft, such as regularly scheduled commercial service. An example would be moving three personnel from II MEF to Italy or Germany on orders (with weapons authorized) to support a joint task force (JTF) that, because of airlift availability, must use scheduled airline service.

Actions at the APOE

Detailed responsibilities of supporting and supported units at the APOE can be found in DODR 4500.9-R, Part I and Part III. Local policy/SOP guides passenger and cargo arrival showtimes at the APOE. The following is typically covered in local directives:

- Showtime at the APOE for supplies and equipment for each aircraft load.
- JI schedule.
- Passenger and baggage showtime at the APOE: troop and baggage transportation from the marshalling area to the staging area will be requested by the moving unit. At the APOE, the MSC embarkation representative will be prepared to turn over the appropriate number of corrected passenger manifests to the DACG. Baggage will be palletized, weighed, and marked (if using AMC aircraft) or weighed and ready for stowage (if using commercial aircraft).
- Showtime for units using OSA: allow enough time for weighing/tagging of baggage and manifesting of personnel 1 hour prior to aircraft departure.

Actual staging/showtimes should be IAW local SOP, but may require adjustment depending on the airflow/situation. Only the AACG/DACG has the authority to adjust required showtimes to accomplish an orderly airlift evolution.

Alert Holding Area/Call Forward Line

This is the DACG's area of responsibility. The alert holding area/call forward line is located at the APOE. Coordinate with the DACG/TALCE on specific location of each area prior to moving units from the marshalling area. The DACG will coordinate with the moving unit's ALE to call forward aircraft chalk loads. The main purpose of this area is to ensure all items to be moved are properly prepared for the JI conducted by representatives of the unit, DACG or TALCE.

Loading Ramp/Ready Line

This is the TALCE's area of responsibility where they receive control of the chalks from the DACG and conduct additional briefings and inspections as required. All responsibilities for movement from this point forward is the responsibility of the USAF. The TALCE will coordinate with the DACG to call forward chalks. The TALCE may require load team augmentation.

JI Procedures

The JI is conducted between the moving unit, DACG, and USAF airlift support personnel. Once the moving unit passes the JI, AMC becomes responsible for the cargo and equipment in that particular chalk. A JI is documented on a DD Form 2133, *Joint Airlift Inspection Record*. Refer to DODR 4500.9-R, Part III for detailed requirements, guidance, and a checklist.

Prior to the presentation of the aircraft load for JI, the following items should be prepared:

- Shipper's declaration of dangerous goods, if applicable.
- Passenger manifest.
- Cargo manifest (load plans) reflecting actual data.
- Shoring/dunnage, if applicable.

CHAPTER 9
REDEPLOYMENT PREPARATIONS

Embarkation personnel and other redeployment planners must be familiar with US Customs Service (USCS) and USDA requirements. When returning from an exercise or operation, embarkation planners must ensure that time is allocated for inspections before redeployment. Embarkation planners should thoroughly review DODR 4500.9-R, *Part V, DOD Customs and Border Clearance Policies and Procedures*, and SECNAVINST 6210.2A/Army Regulation (AR) 40-12/AFR 161-4, *Quarantine Regulations of the Armed Forces* to ensure all USCS and USDA requirements are met.

Customs and Agriculture Inspections Responsibilities

DOD

Headquarters Department of the Army, Assistant Secretary of the Army for Acquisition, Logistics and Technology is the DOD Executive Agent for the Military Customs Inspection Program (MCIP). Under the supervision of the USCS and USDA, the military customs inspector conducts customs and agriculture inspections on personnel and material leaving the overseas theater. Overseas unified commanders are responsible for compliance with DODR 4500.9-R, Part V, which establishes guidelines for processing and shipping DOD-sponsored retrograde material, and DODD 5030.49, *DOD Customs and Border Clearance Program*, which establishes policies and procedures under which USCS and USDA authorize military customs inspectors to inspect material and personnel returning to US customs territory.

Marine Force Component Command (MARFORPAC/MARFORLANT)

MARFORPAC/MARFORLANT receive requests for assistance via the MEFs; e.g., manpower that exceeds organic capabilities.

MEF

The MEF's senior inspector usually has the final military authority during customs/agriculture inspections and washdowns. The ultimate final authority rests with the USCS and USDA.

The MEF usually provides guidance and oversight of MCIP and USDA inspection programs. Typically, the MEF—

- Coordinates external border clearance requirements and provides technical advice on customs/agriculture inspections and agriculture washdowns.

- Provides deploying units with a detailed briefing on customs/agriculture inspections and agriculture washdowns. Resources at this level include applicable references and support from senior inspectors. Senior inspectors may actually come from the FSSG or the supporting establishment (military police for military customs inspectors and the medical battalion; the naval regional medical center or Navy hospital for the Navy entomologist and preventive medicine technicians [PMTs]).

- Receives requests submitted to the senior inspector for inspection teams.

- Budgets and provides funds for the temporary additional duty (TAD) of inspection teams for contingency operations and training exercises.

Deployed MAGTF Command Element and the CSSE

The deployed MAGTF command element (CE) and the CSSE coordinate to—

- Schedule the senior military customs inspector, PMT, and USCS/USDA officials for coordination meetings and briefings.
- Conduct troop information classes by the senior military customs inspector and PMT and USCS/USDA representatives (if available) prior to and during the deployment.
- Identify shortfalls and propose solutions where washdown facilities are inadequate at the proposed final overseas backloading port, base or airport. The deployed MAGTF CE coordinates required support with in-country contacts or liaison agencies. Additional requirements may include fresh water washdown facilities at a final overseas port or site.
- Determine the scope and extent of agriculture washdown requirements based on the amount of equipment and supplies that require washing and inspecting.
- Schedule briefings with the senior inspector, USCS/USDA officials, and appropriate staff members.
- Develop a detailed plan for customs/agriculture inspections and washdown operations.
- Ensure washdown equipment is available.
- Develop and enforce inspection and cleaning procedures.
- Determine equipment and supplies that were not exposed to foreign soil contamination and that will not be offloaded for the washdown. These items should be listed and certified via letter to the senior inspector to be free of contamination.
- Identify potential contamination problems from previous operations concerning backloading equipment, supplies, and vehicles.
- Provide the senior inspector with the required personnel and equipment to include additional inspectors, vehicles, radio operators, and radios for the customs and agriculture inspections and agriculture washdown.

Restricted and Prohibited Articles

US border clearance laws and regulations prohibit the import of certain items or restrict import by placing specific conditions or prescribing quantity limitations. For detailed information and a list of restricted and/or prohibited articles, refer to DODR 4500.9-R, Part V. Every country has unique border clearance laws (customs and agriculture). Many times military customs inspectors are US and host nation officials. It is essential that liaison be established with the host nation or appropriate US representative; e.g., embassy or combatant commander J-4 when planning a deployment to/from a foreign country.

Military Customs Inspection Procedures

Customs inspections usually depend on the mode of transportation used for the redeployment. Units may have resident military customs inspectors who have been certified through military customs inspector training provided by USCS.

Amphibious Shipping

If returning to CONUS via amphibious shipping, units should follow the guidelines listed in MCRP 4-11C.

Airlift

If units are redeploying via air, a military customs inspector, in concert with APOD control agencies, will be responsible for the inspection.

Equipment, Containers, and Vehicles

The military customs inspector will inspect all unit gear prior to pallet buildup. The inspection is usually completed after equipment, containers or boxes to be palletized have completed the washdown process. The militarly customs inspector will then inspect all unit vehicles and stand-alone containers. Unit representatives should be on hand to provide access to any secured containers or boxes as required.

Once the vehicle, pallet or container has been inspected, the item will be tagged with a serialized tag or some other means to ensure that access is secured until the item returns to CONUS.

Before boarding aircraft, the military customs inspector will ensure all personnel are inspected for restricted, prohibited, and controlled items.

Personnel

All personnel will complete a US Customs declaration form. Units will coordinate with the military customs inspector to ensure this requirement is met.

USCS Declaration Forms and Terms

Tariff (Duty) Exemptions for the Armed Forces

There are different tariff (duty) exemptions for different situations. The US Armed Forces are given some unique exemptions not given to a US citizen tourist returning to the customs territory of the US (CTUS). If a military member returns with items acquired abroad that exceed their personal exemption, he must pay the appropriate tariff (duty). Tariffs range from 2 to 35 percent and are subject to change.

Customs Territory

All vessels and aircraft arriving from ports outside of the CTUS must be cleared by the USCS. The CTUS is defined as the 50 States, the District of Columbia, and Puerto Rico.

Extended Duty

All members of the US Armed Forces serving on naval vessels are considered to be permanently deployed if they—

- Have served on the vessel for 120 days outside of the CTUS.
- Left the CTUS with the intention of serving on a vessel for 120 days.

Nonresident Exemption

Any military member serving outside of the CTUS on an extended duty deployment may claim the status of nonresident when returning to the CTUS for a short visit (more than 72 hours), provided that he intends to return to his duty station abroad. This includes leave and TAD.

Customs Declaration

The USCS requires that all articles acquired abroad be declared in writing. For a complete list of customs terms and phrases, see DODR 4500.9-R, Part V.

USDA Washdowns

The purpose of an agriculture washdown and certification is to prevent introducing harmful public health or agricultural agents from entering the US on military equipment. SECNAVINST 6210.2A/ AR 40-12/AFR161-4 describes DOD support for the United States Public Health Service and the USDA to prevent such introductions. This reference prohibits the redeployment of vehicles and cargo from a foreign country unless they are free of animal, pest, and soil contamination.

Planning

Detailed planning and logistical forethought must be given to selecting the washdown site and ensuring sufficient supplies and equipment are available to conduct the washdown. Planning should culminate in a backload/washdown conference to be attended by all participating commands and inspectors.

During planning emphasis should be placed on organization and training of washdown crews. Drivers and assistant drivers must understand the importance of remaining with assigned vehicles and accessory vehicle items throughout the washdown. This will ensure timely movement of vehicles and security of accessory vehicle items and cargo. Detailed organizational planning combined with training should result in a suitable washdown crew schedule with adequate NCO supervision at each washdown point.

To assist in preparing further agriculture inspections, planners work with embarkation personnel to isolate material that was not exposed to contamination, and verify it as such. The material is then segregated in the holds on specific cargo areas using wire screening or ropes to separate it from materials that have gone ashore.

Inspectors may check these areas during the early stages of agriculture washdowns to ensure they are free of all dirt, debris, fruit, beverage cans, etc.

Selecting and Equipping a Washdown Location

A washdown location requires specific physical facilities for effective cleaning and inspection of all supplies and equipment. In addition, a military inspector familiar with USDA requirements with previous washdown experience should be consulted and included on reconnaissance trips to prospective washdown locations. Care should be taken to consider the potential adverse impact of the washdown operation and to minimize effects of used (gray) water and contaminants on the local environment.

Note: Refer to MCRP 4-11C for information on conducting a washdown with amphibious shipping backloads and redeployments.

Hardstand

The availability of hardstand is one of the major limiting factors in how long a washdown takes. Hardstand is a hard surface which, even when wet, will not allow any soil to be transferred to vehicles, supplies, and equipment. Areas where hardstand is absolutely essential are those associated with the actual washing of vehicles; those used for offloading and cleaning the vehicle accessory items; staging areas for clean vehicles awaiting backload, and all roads in between the above areas.

When inspecting the hardstand area, consider the run-off of wash water into marine environments. Any fuel or other contaminants from the vehicles being washed may go directly into such an environment causing harm to shellfish or other marine life.

Evaluate the need for berms or other containment strategies and the possibility of reutilizing the runoff water.

Washdown areas for vehicles and equipment cleaning/staging areas for cargo and mobile loads should support all phases of the washdown and inspection process. A clean vehicle staging area should be established, capable of staging clean, inspected gear, based on the expected pace of the backload operation.

Fresh Water Availability

Large quantities of fresh water (**salt water will corrode vehicles**) are consumed quickly during washdown operations. Approximately 250,000 gallons are required for an average MEU (2,400 personnel and related equipment) with 300 wheeled vehicles using two 1/2-inch fire hoses operating at the minimum recommended pressure of 90 pounds per square inch (psi).

In many areas only gray water is available. Gray water is defined as nonsaline, but with a number of contaminants from prior use. Though not used for sewage purposes, storage of this water and the absence of chlorine make it a potential disease carrier for those in close contact with it during the washing operations. Basic immunizations are recommended.

In addition to the amount of water required/available, consider the adequacy of the water pressure.

Environmental Considerations

Assess the potential adverse impact of the agriculture washdown and take all reasonable actions to minimize effects of used water and contaminants on the local environment. Contaminants must be captured and removed to authorized collection areas.

Washrack Requirements

The design and number of washracks will largely determine the speed at which the agriculture washdown can be conducted.

Design the washracks for safely placing vehicles on and off the rack while maintaining unrestricted access to all vehicle surfaces for the cleaning personnel. Adequate working clearance between the bottom of the vehicle and the ground is essential because the undercarriage of each vehicle must be washed, inspected, and if necessary, rewashed and reinspected before being allowed off the washrack. If the vehicle is too close to the ground, the efficiency of the work crews and the inspection/rewash process would be greatly hampered, considerably extending the washdown time.

The number of washracks required will vary with the amount of time available. Historically, the agriculture washdown proceeds at an average rate of one vehicle per individual washrack per hour of daylight.

A person should be designated to guide the vehicles up and down the washracks to maintain a safe throughput rate.

Water Pump Requirements

The design, output, and reliability of pumps can affect the speed of a washdown operation.

Provide a minimum of two hose lines for each individual washrack. The pumps should be capable of sustaining a minimum output pressure of 90 psi for many hours of continuous use.

Fire department pumper trucks will work well and are usually available at any seaport, airport or military base. Several hose lines with 90 psi outputs can be routinely operated off a single truck.

A supply of new hoses should be kept in reserve.

Agriculture Washdown Equipment

Prior planning is necessary to determine requirements and request appropriate support when working overseas. Coordination and assistance will be required from the host facility/nation. Equipment recommended for a successful washdown is listed in table 9-1. This list requires modification based on the unit size, the washdown location, and available host nation support.

All locks on compartments, boxes, tool chests, and other locked items will need to be removed before inspection. If keys cannot be found, provisions should be made to cut the locks.

Proper tools, any tire irons, wrenches, special screwdrivers or other required tools need to be available to remove dual tires, gun mounts, plates, and floor mat bolts on different vehicles.

Table 9-1. Equipment for Successful Washdown.

EQUIPMENT	QTY
Vehicle washracks	4
Flooding set	6
Rough terrain forklift	4
Cranes	As required
Air compressor	2
Water truck (5,000 gal)	1
Water tank (3,000 gal) or SIXCONS	2; 7 - 8
Flatbed trucks to move supplies	As required
Pump (55 gal. per minute or greater)	2
"Y" gates	3
Fire hose (1 1/2"), 600'	2 per washrack

Table 9-1. Equipment Items for Successful Washdown (Continued).

EQUIPMENT	QTY
Fire hose (2 1/2"), 200'	2 per washrack
Fire nozzles (2 per washrack)	8
Steam jenny	Minimum 2 (as required)
Steam manifold (6 stations)	1
Steam hose (1/2", 12')	6
Steam hose (1 1/2"), 300'	1
Cold/wet weather clothing	40 sets (assorted sizes)
Hard hats	40
Rubber gloves	20 Pair (assorted sizes)
Rubber boots	15 Pair (assorted sizes)
Safety goggles	40
Ear plugs	Box
Flashlights and batteries	24
Straw brooms	40
Putty knives	200
Small flat bladed screwdrivers	Minimum 12 (to clean tracks)
Steel rod (5 feet)	12
Wire brushes	100
Scrub brushes	100
Rags	As required
Garden hose/nozzles	75'
Vacuum cleaner (wet/dry) (as required for aircraft and vehicles)	Minimum 6
Waterless hand cleaner	Equivalent of 1 gal
Portable head	1 per 25 persons daily (varies)

Agriculture Inspectors

Military inspectors usually consist of at least one Navy entomologist and a number of PMTs sourced by the MEF from the FSSG's medical battalion, the naval regional medical center or Navy hospital. Military inspectors must maintain strict compliance with USDA guidelines to ensure an unhindered and timely reentry approval into CONUS by USDA and US Public Health Service officials.

Military inspectors will vary depending on their branch of Service. Navy Medical Department PMTs are certified through Bureau of Medicine and Surgery Instruction (BUMEDINST) 6250.12C, *Pesticide Applicator Training and Certification for Medical Personnel*. Normally PMT's work for/with the Navy entomologist. *All military inspectors*, also called USDA military cooperators, serve at the discretion of the USDA. Marines can fall under this category after completing training provided by the USDA. Military inspectors—

- Establish necessary administrative requirements. USDA officials review these administrative requirements and conduct any final inspections that may be required at the point of entry.
- Attach inspection certification tags to each vehicle after cleaning/inspection has been completed.
- Maintain an inspection log to track the number of vehicles and to insure a double check for the tagged vehicles.

USDA Inspections

Cleaning equipment when redeploying and conducting an agriculture inspection overseas do not preclude a USDA plant protection and quarantine program inspection upon return to CONUS. The USDA can require this additional inspection. However, close coordination with the USDA usually results in no further inspections or delays at the CONUS port of entry.

Rigid USDA inspection standards allow only a thin film of road dust on vehicles and equipment at the CONUS final port of entry. Because of these stringent standards, inspections of vehicles and equipment will be conducted only during daylight hours. Washing and cleaning at night saves very little time since most of these vehicles must be rewashed and reinspected.

Washing Standards

Standards differ based on the degree that vehicles, containers, and equipment were exposed to contaminants. Vehicles typically get washed prior to reembarkation aboard ship after an operation or exercise. Cleanliness of equipment enroute to the final washdown location aboard amphibious shipping will range from lightly soiled to heavily contaminated. In this case a limited washdown will typically satisfy USDA requirements. For units that deployed overseas using Military Sealift Command shipping or AMC aircraft and whose equipment had prolonged exposure to contaminants, a more rigorous washdown is required.

Limited Washdown

A limited washdown may be conducted on vehicles and equipment that had minimum exposure to the environment during operations and where such exposure would be harmless from the standpoint of agricultural or public health concerns. The most common example is road dirt or dust from traveling on a hard surface road or highway.

Ships

Cleaning of all stowage areas for vehicles or equipment that were contaminated is required. This includes cleaning soil from recessed areas of the decks; e.g., clover leafs, pad eyes, and tie-down channels, and under shelving from corners and other hard-to-reach areas). Lower decks on certain amphibious ships can be submerged in salt water to satisfactorily eliminate contamination problems.

Large Aircraft

For aircraft that operated from a hard surface airfield, protected areas such as wheel wells and around cargo or passenger doors are cleaned. Cargo and flight deck are visually inspected and cleaned if necessary.

Amphibious Vehicles and Landing Craft

For AAVs; lighter, amphibious, resupply, cargo, 5-ton (LARC-Vs); landing craft air cushion (LCAC); and landing crafts, utility (LCUs), the troop compartment, crew area, and the crew's personal equipment are cleaned. Ensure other areas are exposed to salt water during operation. If vehicles washed with salt water are to be transported on aircraft, all salt water must be removed or contained to prevent contamination of aircraft with corrosive salt solutions that can seriously damage airframes.

Comprehensive Washdown

This level of washdown is accomplished for vehicles, equipment, and supplies exposed to contamination during sustained operations ashore. Supplies and equipment mobile-loaded on contaminated vehicles are offloaded. Accessory items and palletized supplies are staged in a pest-free area for cleaning. Vehicles proceed to a steam or washing station as determined by inspectors. Upon final inspection, material from mobile loads is reloaded aboard vehicles and the clean vehicles and supplies are re-embarked.

Fixed- and Rotary-Wing Aircraft

The cabin area, cockpit, wheels, wheel wells, skid/runner bars, under deck plates, panels, in flap wells, other areas where foreign soil may have lodged, and personal equipment of crew and pilot are cleaned.

Ground Vehicles

Cleaning motor vehicles usually consumes the greatest amount of time and causes the most delays. Before arrival at the washrack—

- Sweep or vacuum the vehicle cab and all storage and tool compartments.
- Remove the battery, clean it and the battery box, replace the battery.

- Remove the outside dual wheels and spare tires; place in the back for later cleaning at the washrack.
- Remove all padlocks, seat cushions, detachable sideboards, canvas sides/tops, and any personal gear brought ashore; leave at the mobile load staging area.
- Handpick or sweep any grass or vegetation from the radiator.
- Let down the sides of all trucks that are equipped with collapsible sides.
- Scrub and scrape.

At the washrack, vehicles will be hosed down with high pressure (recommend minimum 90 psi) fresh water or steam (steam may remove valuable protective coatings) paying particular attention to undercarriages, fender wells, axles, springs, bumpers, wheels, and recessed areas. As a corrosion prevention measure, salt water is not used for cleaning vehicles. Inspect each vehicle thoroughly to ensure that all soil is removed, using a flashlight, screwdriver or putty knife where necessary. The following are common problem areas that cause backups at the inspection checkpoints:

- Topside access areas:
  - Floor boards.
  - Battery box.
  - All storage/tool compartments.
  - Motor compartments.
  - Wheels and tires.
  - Windshield base (folding windshield).
  - Front and rear bumper hollows and braces.
  - Radiator front.
  - Truck beds.
  - All other spaces where soil might be found.
- Underside access areas:
  - Fender wells (front and rear) including access openings for tail light wiring.
  - Rocker panels.
  - Frame (fore and aft).
  - Coil spring wells (front and rear).

- Transmission support beam.
- Rear suspension A-frame (pivot points and drain holes).
- Trailer hitch bolt recess.
- Front, side, and rear body lips.
- Drive shaft tunnel.
- Power take-offs.
- Axle brackets.
- Fuel tanks (between body and tank).
- Transaxle brackets.
- Leaf springs.
- Air tank braces.
- Drain and access holes.
- Universal joint between body parts.

Tracked Vehicles

Cleaning tracked vehicles is by far the most difficult and time consuming. It is strongly recommended that cleaning on board ship be accomplished as soon as possible after the final contingency operation or exercise because of the excessive amount of time required to properly clean. All soil impacted in the treads, around the rubber cleats, in the tread connectors, between and behind tread guides and roller supports, and all other spaces must be removed. Interiors must be soil-free, including the battery box. The bilges may contain some sand, but only if it is mixed with salt water. If tracked vehicles are to be transported on aircraft, all salt water must be removed or contained to prevent contamination of aircraft with corrosive salt solution. Tracked vehicles may be cleaned in the ship's well deck if enough space for one complete revolution of tread is available. Tracked vehicles may be cleaned on shore only if they can be backloaded without recontaminating the treads.

Cleaning of Supplies and Equipment

Thoroughly clean embarkation boxes, field desks, communications equipment, and similar items with hand brooms, rags, and other nonwater methods.

Give specific attention to cracks, crevices, and recesses. Personnel must clean pallets and loads of compacted soil and vegetation. Padlocked boxes must also be inspected so responsible personnel with keys must be standing by to open them or locks will be cut to access the boxes.

Camouflage nets are difficult to properly clean. Hand cleaning, although time consuming, is the most effective method.

Spread out tents and canvas on a pest-free surface and sweep down on both sides (no water); pay attention to seam and flaps.

Take ashore only essential personal gear during the washdown. Personal gear will not be inspected at the washdown site. However, all personal gear taken ashore is considered contaminated and will be cleaned and subject to an inspection.

Individual weapons will be inspected by unit commanders or authorized representatives.

APPENDIX A
TIME-PHASED FORCE AND DEPLOYMENT DATA

The JOPES database tool, TPFDD, is used to register all strategic sea and air movement requirements to USTRANSCOM for deployments. The unit's operations section (S-3) has overall responsibility for TPFDD management and accuracy. However, as logisticians and the unit's subject matter experts for transportation and deployment preparations, embarkation personnel must be familiar with TPFDD as they will provide UDLs, recommendations, and expertise to support TPFDD development and execution.

TPFDD Development and Execution Process

This appendix provides a basic understanding of TPFDD, its development and execution, and reports used to support FDP&E.

TPFDD development begins with mission analysis and determining force structure to satisfy mission requirements. TPFDD provides the following information:

- In-place forces (units already deployed).
- Forces deployed to support the OPLAN with a priority indicating the phased sequence for their arrival at the POD/destination.
- Routing of forces to be deployed.
- Movement data associated with deploying forces.
- Estimates of nonunit related cargo and personnel movements to be conducted concurrently with force deployment.
- Estimated transportation requirements that must be fulfilled by common-user lift resources and requirements that can be fulfilled by assigned or attached transportation assets.

Responsibilities

TPFDD development is typically accomplished at the MSC level, generally in the steps listed below. The responsible staff section for each step is indicated in parentheses.

Note: TPFDD planning actions are carried out by the MAGTF planners, MOS 0511, Enlisted MAGTF Planning Specialist, and MOS 0502 [skill designator] MAGTF Plans/Operations Officers (when assigned) in the operations/plans section.

- Receive and analyze mission. Establish and monitor news group messages in GCCS and activate the operational planning team (operations/plans section).
- Develop CONOPS. Develop preliminary CONOPS, restatement of mission, and hardcopy tasking to execute mission (operations/plans section).
- Determine requirements. Perform initial force and sustainment sizing and conduct transportation capability study. The JTF is activated along with crisis action teams (operations/plans section; the crisis action team normally falls under its cognizance and is augmented by representatives from the other staff sections).
- Phase deployment flow. Provide commanders estimate, issue warning orders, and develop/refine requirements (operations section).
- Source requirements. From ULN blocks assigned by HHQ, develop ULN force structure shell for units needed to satisfy mission requirements in MAGTF/JFRG II (operations/plans section). Source forces by uploading MDSS II UDLs (provided by embarkation section) into the TPFDD ULN structure for deploying units using MAGTF II and inputting numbers of personnel planned to

deploy for each unit. Forward unsourced requirements to HHQs and distribute deployment orders upon receipt from the issuing authority (operations/plans section).

- Tailor requirements. Refine (embarkation and operations/plans sections) and forward actual lift requirements based on unit MDSS II UDL data and make phasing adjustments (operations/plans section).
- Verify/certify/validate movement requirements. *Verify* and consolidate requirements (MSC/MEF operations/plans section), *verify* TPFDD level IV information (MSC/MEF embarkation section), *certify* transportation requirements (MARFOR operations/plans and strategic mobility office), and (combatant commander) *validate* requirements to USTRANSCOM.
- Allocate (USTRANSCOM) PAX and cargo ULNs to air and sealift carriers; assign lift (AMC/Military Sealift Command); publish movement schedules and conduct load planning (MSC logistics and embarkation section/ MARFOR strategic mobility office).
- Marshal and move to POE. Marshal forces for movement, move to POE, and monitor movement (logistics and embarkation sections).
- Manifest and move to POD. Execute deployment; report departures and arrivals at POE/POD to the LMCC (logistics and embarkation section) and manifest *actual* PAX and cargo S/Ts for ULNs in the TFPDD (operations/plans section).
- Receive loads at POD and move to final destination (embarkation and logistics sections).

ULN Structuring

A ULN is a seven-character alphanumeric code that describes a unique increment of a unit deployment, i.e., advance party, main body, equipment by sea and air, reception team, or trail party, in a JOPES TPFDD (JP 1-02). It is made up of three elements: a force requirement number (FRN), a fragmentation code (FRAG), and an insert code (INSERT). The ULN is much like a

landing serial number for an amphibious operation in that it uniquely identifies a movement requirement. The following list contains some specifics that will assist in preliminary ULN structuring. The ULN structure should be provided by the MAGTF planners in the operations section via the TPFDD LOI.

- Consists of personnel, vehicles, equipment, and cargo from the same unit/same UIC.
- "Moves" from the same origin to the same destination via the same POE, POD, and intermediate locations.
- Moves during a specific movement window.
- Moves by the same mode and source.
- There is **no** standard allocation procedure. Each combatant commander and Service component command; e.g., MARFORLANT and MARFORPAC, have unique allocation procedures.

TPFDD Working Paper Reports and Data Elements

Knowledge of the kinds of data in the TPFDD and how the data can be packaged in "standard" or ad hoc reports is critical to verify and validate a unit's movement requirements. Three commonly used reports are the summary of forces and deployment data working paper (F11D); the time-phased transportation requirements working paper (F11E-TON(TN) and F11E-SQUARE(SQ), and the cargo detail working paper report (F11W).

Summary of Forces and Deployment Data Working Paper (F11D)

The F11D provides a summary of movement requirements, POD, and destination data. The F11D is in aggregated level (*Level I cargo detail*) (less measurement tons (MTONS) to include the total number of PAX and S/Ts to be moved. The F11D is one of the most common reports. Some of the embarkation related data fields are duplicated in the F11W and described in F11W section below. The F11D can be customized and sorted to produce an ad hoc report based on user-defined parameters; e.g., service, mode, and source.

Unit Name (30 Characters)

Remember the force description describes the unit generally; e.g., Rifle Co, Infantry Bn. The *unit name* describes the unit *specifically*; e.g., "A" Co, 1/8. JOPES automatically sources the unit name from the UIC file in the global status of resources and training system (GSORTS). Changes can be made once the JOPES unit name is imported into the record.

UIC (Six Characters)

This six-character alphanumeric code uniquely identifies each active, reserve, and National Guard unit of the Armed Forces. There are many sources for finding the UIC; e.g., AC/S G-4 supply officer/maintenance management officer or AC/S G-3/G-5 plans/GCCS operator.

Unit Type Code (Five Characters)

The unit type code (UTC) is an alphanumeric code that uniquely identifies each type unit in the Armed Forces. The UTC is the look-up field within the type unit characteristics (TUCHA) file. The TUCHA is a file that gives standard planning data and movement characteristics for personnel, cargo, and accompanying supplies associated with deployable type units of fixed composition. The file contains the weight and volume of selected cargo categories, physical characteristics of the cargo and the number of personnel requiring nonorganic transportation. The TUCHA is maintained at the Service headquarters; i.e., HQMC level. Examples of type units are a rifle company, FA-18 squadron or an artillery battery. There are also task-organized detachments listed

in the TUCHA; e.g., MAGTFs or MAGTF detachments. If you have questions about the TUCHA, see MAGTF planning personnel (MOS 05XX) in the unit's operations or plans section.

Parent Indicator Code (One Character)

The parent indicator code (PIC) is used by MAGTF planners to define the ULN's parent status.

Service Code (One Character)

If a MARFOR, the Service code (SVC) is "M."

Providing Organization Code (One Character))

Example
For I MEF forces (assigned to the combatant commander, US Pacific Command) the providing organization code is "5."

Authorized Number of Personnel/PAX

The number of PAX authorized to move and the number planned to move.

Total S/Ts/Cubic Feet Bulk or Barrels

Provides a rollup of total cargo short tons, bulk stowed items; e.g; grains or liquids, packaged in barrels.

Location Name POD/Destination

The geographic point (aerial or seaport) in the routing scheme where a movement requirement will complete its strategic deployment.

Earliest Arrival Date

The earliest arrival date (EAD) is a day relative to C-day when a unit can be accepted at the POD during a deployment. Used with the latest arrival date (LAD), it defines a delivery window for transportation planning.

LAD/RDD

LAD/RDD is days relative to C-day (see *Dates* paragraph below), when a unit can arrive at the POD and support the CONOPS/when a unit must arrive at its destination and complete unloading.

Mode POD/Destination (Dest) and Source (SRC) Code

Indicates the modes and sources of transportation planned to move the unit to the POD and destination. See table A-1.

Table A-1. Mode and Source Codes.

CODE	MEANING
AC	Air via supporting commander channel (AMC or Service aircraft)
AD	Air via theater (supported commander) aircraft
AH	Air via organic (unit) aircraft
AK	Air via strategic (AMC, AMC-contract) aircraft
AL	Air via AMC, Government PAX/commercial ticket program
AM	Air via unit-funded commercial tickets
AN	Air via host nation/allied provided airlift
AS	Air via SAAM
LD	Land via theater (supported commander) rail
LG	Land via SDDC-arranged trucking or rail
LH	Land via organic (unit) vehicles
LR	Land via theater (supported commander) trucking
LN	Land via host nation/allied controlled transport
PC	Mode optional; source is supporting combatant commander (to other than a CONUS SPOE)
PG	Mode optional; source is SDDC (CONUS only)
SC	Sea via USN/USCG ship
SD	Sea via USN/USCG ship (MPS)
SE	Sea via Military Sealift Command ship (common user strategic sealift)
SH	Sea via organic (unit) vessels
SN	Sea via host nation/allied provided sealift
SP	Sea/canal via barge/ferry
SW	Sea via Military Sealift Command (assault follow-on echelon)
XG	No transportation required (origin and POE same; CONUS SPOEs)
XX	No transportation required (origin and POE or POD and destination same)
Z (blank)	Requirement is in place at its final destination

Dates

All dates in TPFDD and working paper reports are based upon C-day or N-day.

C-day is the unnamed day on which deployment for an operation commences or is to commence; established by a combatant commander or higher. (C-day is C000; day *after* C-day is C001).

N-day is an unnamed day before C-day when a unit is notified for deployment or redeployment. (Day *before* C-day is N001).

Time-Phased Transportation Requirements Working Paper (F11E-TON(TN) and F11E-SQUARE(SQ)

The F11E-TN provides a listing showing planned itinerary and summary cargo data of total PAX, S/Ts, and MTONS (*Level II cargo detail*) for each unit. The F11E-SQ (*Level III detail*) provides a complete list showing planned itinerary and summary cargo data indicating an organization's total PAX and square foot stowage requirement. Like the F11D and the F11W, the F11E's output can also be adjusted to create an ad hoc report based on user defined parameters. Level II is rolled up from Levels III and IV (see Levels of Detail, appendix M).

Cargo Detail Working Paper Report (F11W)

The F11W provides a list of Level IV cargo detail data for each CCC to be moved by a unit. Its Level IV information is combined with the planned transportation routing requirements and geographic codes (GEOCODEs) to provide a complete picture of the cargo, vehicles, and equipment the organization needs to move and how those items will be transported to the final destination. The F11W's data fields listed on page A-6 identify CCC information, locations, dates, etc. required for movement.

The CCC is a three character alphanumeric code that identifies movement characteristics and the type of wheeled/tracked vehicle or cargo item identified as a lift requirement. CCCs have many possible character combinations. Planners must think of how the cargo can be configured and physically transported and what the desired mode of transportation is. Each cargo item can have only one CCC. Choose the one that best describes the unit's movement requirement. For example, a HMMWV can be coded as an R2B, R2C or R2D; a bulldozer an A1D or A2D; bulk HAZMAT (lithium batteries) D3A, D3B, D3C or D3D; and general supplies as J3A, J3B, J3C or J3D. Tables A-2 through A-4 provide explanations for each character. The first character of the CCC categorizes the item to be moved.

Table A-2. First Character of CCC.

CODE	MEANING
A	All wheeled and tracked vehicles (self-propelled or towed) that are neither security nor hazardous cargo (see codes K and L below) and are not suitable for road marching for overland deployment legs.
B	Uncrated non-self deployment aircraft (NSDA). If self-deployable aircraft will not be deployed under their own power, they must be identified as NSDA and their force movement characteristics reported.
C	Floating craft.
D	Hazardous nonvehicular cargo (see code E below).
E	Security nonvehicular cargo or nonvehicular cargo that is both security and hazardous.
F	Cargo requiring refrigeration by mover.
G	Bulk POL, not packaged.
H	Bulk granular cargo; e.g., crushed rock or sand.
J	Other nonvehicular cargo, including packaged POL, crated aircraft, technical assistance team yellow.
K	Vehicle designated as security cargo or both security cargo and hazardous cargo.
L	Vehicles designated as hazardous cargo, but no security cargo.
M	Ammunition.
N	Nuclear weapons.
P	Chemical munitions.
R	All wheeled and tracked vehicles (self-propelled or towed) that are neither security nor hazardous cargo and are suitable for road march for overland deployment legs and capable of convoy speeds up to 40 mph.

The second character indicates if cargo is unit equipment, accompanying unit supply, non-unit cargo, transportable by air or is prepositioned.

Table A-3. Second Character of CCC.

UNIT EQUIP-MENT	ACCOMPA-NIED UNIT SUPPLY	NON-UNIT CARGO	MEANING
0	4	A	Nonair transportable cargo: exceeds any of the dimensions 1453" x 216" or has a height between 114" and 156" and wider than exceeds 144". All dimensions are expressed in length x width x height. Width and height pertain to aircraft door limitations.
1	5	B	Outsized cargo: exceeds 1090" x 117" x 105" and is qualified by MILSTAMP aircraft air dimension code (too large for C-130/C-141).
2	6	C	Oversized cargo: exceeds the usable dimension of a 463L pallet (104" x 84" x 96") or height as established by the cargo envelope of the particular model of aircraft.
3	7	D	Bulk cargo: dimension less than those of oversize cargo.
8	9		Organic cargo: Non-TCC cargo is prepositioned or will be transported via organic sources and does not require TCC support.

The third character indicates if a vehicle organic to the unit transports cargo or if cargo can and/or will be containerized.

Table A-4. Third Character of CCC.

CODE	MEANING
A	Cargo is normally carried on a vehicle that is organic to the unit (N/A to non-unit related cargo).
B	Cargo can be containerized, meets the dimensional criteria for 20-foot container (231" x 92" x 84") and does not exceed a weight of 20 short tons. For vehicles being shipped in 20-foot containers, maximum dimensions are 225" x 84" x 82". These dimensions allow space for blocking and bracing, etc.
C	Cargo can be containerized, does not meet the dimensional criteria for 20-foot container, but does meet dimensional criteria for a 40-foot container (472.5" x 92" x 84") and does not exceed a weight of 40 short tons. For vehicles being shipped in 40-foot containers, maximum dimensions are 468" x 84" x 86". These dimensions allow space for blocking and bracing, etc.
D	Cargo cannot or will not be containerized.

PAX

APERS (authorized personnel) and NRPAX (number PAX).

Dimensions

The length, width, and height in inches.

PCS

Number of pieces—quantity.

Square Feet

The total square foot lift requirement for the organization. If length and width are entered, the system will calculate the square feet.

S/Ts (2,000 pounds)

The S/Ts for each individual item. The system will multiply by number of pieces - quantity (PCS), and display totals on the top line roll-up. S/Ts are categorized as either bulk (BULK(ST)), oversized (OVER(ST)), or outsized (OUT(ST)) based upon the CCC.

MTONS

If length, width, and height are entered, the system will calculate the MTONS (total cubic foot divided by 40, where 40 cubic foot = 1 MTON). As for S/Ts, MTONS are categorized as either bulk (BULK[MT]), oversized (OVER[MT]) or outsized (OUT[MT]) based on the CCC.

Origin

The beginning point of deployment; the point or station where a movement requirement is located. JOPES automatically sources the origin GEO-CODE of the UIC automatically from GSORTS. Changes may be made after the GSORTS origin

GEOCODE is imported into the record. GEOCODEs can be found from the look-up option for that field in the in current LOGAIS. Examples of GEOCODEs:

- ETFB Camp Lejeune, NC.
- ETZB Marine Corps Base (MCB) Camp Pendleton, CA.
- SBDJ Norfolk, VA.

POE

The geographic point (air or seaport GEOCODE) in the routing scheme where a movement requirement will begin its strategic deployment.

Intermediate Location

An intermediate stopping point (GEOCODE) in the deployment routing of a unit could be used to identify any layover that may be required for a specified time, normally longer than 1 day. It is often used to unite the personnel and cargo of a split shipment. This point may occur between the origin and POE, the POE and POD or the POD and destination.

POD

The geographic point (port or airfield GEOCODE) in the routing scheme where a movement requirement will complete its strategic deployment.

Destination

The terminal geographic location (GEOCODE) in the routing scheme for forces only (sustainment and replacement personnel are routed to a port of support). The destination identifies the station or location in the objective area where the unit will be employed. For some units, the destination may be the same as their POD.

Mode Code (M) and Source Codes (S)

One character each (see table A-1, page A-4).

RLD

A date, relative to C-day when a unit will be ready to move from the origin, i.e., mobilization.

ALD

A date, relative to C-day, specified for each unit in a TPFDD indicating when that unit will be ready to load at the POE.

EAD

A day, relative to C-day, that is the earliest date when a unit, a resupply shipment or replacement personnel can be accepted at the POD during a deployment. Used with the LAD, it defines a delivery window for transportation planning.

LAD

A day, relative to C-day, that is the latest date when a unit, a resupply shipment or replacement personnel can arrive at the POD and support the CONOPS. Used with the EAD, it defines a delivery window for transportation planning.

RDD

A date, relative to C-day, when a unit must arrive at its destination and complete unloading to enable it to support the CONOPS.

Combatant Commander's Required Date

The original date specified by the geographic combatant commander for arrival of forces or cargo at the destination; used in the TPFDD to assess the impact of a later arrival.

APPENDIX B
TURNOVER FOLDERS AND DESKTOP PROCEDURES

A turnover folder contains pertinent information about a key billet which, when passed on to any individual newly assigned to the billet, allows him to assume duties in a minimum amount of time. Recommended content includes (but is not limited to) the following:

- Letter or special order assigning the individual to the billet (if required).
- Organizational chart.
- Billet description.
- Functional areas of responsibility.
- Special duties and tasks.
- A copy of pertinent references.
- POC by command, billet, grade, name, telephone number, and e-mail address. Embarkation representatives will have a POC list of two levels higher and all subordinate units.
- Problem areas sufficiently defined.
- Status of pending projects.
- Required reports and reporting procedures.
- Past inspection results, reports of corrective action taken on inspection discrepancies, if any, and internal inspection procedures.
- Copy of a SAAM request. A sample SAAM and submission requirements will be included.

- Copy of garrison UDL.
- Garrison UDL procedures.
- List of unit/section lift requirements and HAZMAT.
- Internal/external movement support request procedures to obtain MHE, vehicles, and buses.
- Copies of all outstanding embarkation box construction requests.
- Copy of requesting procedures for 463L pallets and associated equipment.
- Copies of appointment letters for all embarkation billet holders.

Desktop procedures list procedures, references, and other related information on managing the functional areas of a particular billet. These procedures define in writing the routine functioning (who, what, when, where, why, and how) of a billet. This file is an integral part of the turnover folder. Desktop procedures should include, but are not limited to, the following:

- A brief description of the duties and responsibilities of assigned personnel.
- A summary of the daily routine.
- Descriptions or charts that reflect the routine flow of paper or work.
- Work priorities within the section or office.

APPENDIX C
UNIT INSPECTION DOCUMENTATION EXAMPLES

Date

MEMORANDUM

From: Battalion Embarkation NCO
To: Section Embarkation Representatives

Subj: EMBARKATION READINESS INSPECTION

1. On (date), there will be an embarkation readiness inspection of all subordinate sections in the battalion. All embarkation representatives are required to be present during the inspection of their section.

2. All discrepancies noted will be corrected and reinspection will be conducted on (date, to be determined but not later than 30 days after initial inspection).

3. POC concerning this matter is (Embark NCO) at extension 1234.

(Embark NCO)

MEMORANDUM

From: Battalion Embarkation NCO
To: Battalion Embarkation Officer

Subj: RESULTS OF EMBARKATION READINESS INSPECTION HELD ON (DATE)

1. The following is a list of discrepancies noted:

SECTION	DISCREPANCIES
S-3	- Insufficient number of 6-cube boxes on hand to embark for movement.
	- Incorrect weight markings on boxes 0305, 0321, and 0325.
SUPPLY	- Insufficient number of pallets and pallet boards for tents.
	- Water cans not properly marked or palletized.
MOTOR TRANSPORT	- Vehicle serial numbers 123456, 654321, and 918273 missing unit designator markings.

2. A reinspection will be held on (date) at the following times:

SECTION	TIME/DATE
S-3	0800, (DATE)
SUPPLY	1000, (DATE)
MOTOR TRANSPORT	1300, (DATE)

POC is (Embark NCO) at extension 1234.

(Embark NCO)

MEMORANDUM

From: Battalion Embarkation NCO
To: Battalion Embarkation Officer

Subj: CORRECTIVE ACTION TAKEN UPON EMBARKATION READINESS
        REINSPECTION

Discrepancies noted on (date) during the embarkation readiness reinspection were corrected with the following exception:

   - Pallets and banding wire for water cans not on order.

(Embark NCO)

APPENDIX D
SAMPLE MSC CGRI CHECKLIST

ORGANIZATION/UNIT: _____

TYPE OF EVALUATION: _____

RATING: _____

INSPECTORS: _____

	T/O Number	Rank/Number Rated	Assigned
0430 Billet Assignments?	1234	W1/1	1
0431 Billet Assignments?	1234	SSgt/1	0

TRAINING	YES	NO	N/A
Has the embarkation officer attended the TEO/assistant course?			
Has the embarkation chief attended the TEO and the logistics embarkation career course?			
Is the embarkation officer certified in air movement planning?			
Is the embarkation chief/clerk certified in air movement planning?			
Is the embarkation officer/chief/clerk certified and current in HAZMAT certification?			
Is the unit conducting on-job-training and sustainment training IAW MCO 1510.61C, *Individual Training Standards (ITS) System for Embarkation/Logistics Occupational Field 04*?			
Have quotas for formal embarkation training been requested for personnel requiring such training?			
REFERENCE MATERIAL			
Does the embarkation section have *access to*—			
- Unit T/O?			
- Unit T/E/unit equipment report (UER)?			
- DODR 4500.9-R, *Defense Transportation Regulation*, Parts I through IV?			
- JP 3-02, *Joint Doctrine for Amphibious Operations*?			
- JP 3-02.2, *Joint Doctrine for Amphibious Embarkation*?			
- MCWP 3-31.5, *Ship-to-Shore Movement*?			
- MCWP 5-1, *Marine Corps Planning Process*?			
- MCRP 5-12D, *Organization of Marine Corps Forces*?			
- MCO P4030.19H, *Preparing Hazardous Materials for Military Air Shipment*?			
- MARFORLANTO 4035.2/4035.1, *Tactical Marking Procedures for Equipment and Embarkation Containers*?			
- FMFLANTO P3120.15A, *SOP for MAGTF Deployments*?			
- MCRP 3-31B, *Amphibious Ships and Landing Craft Data Book*?			
- Landing Force Sixth Fleet SOP?			
- Appropriate division/wing/FSSG/MEF headquarters group SOP?			
- Appropriate MEU SOP?			
- SLCP as required?			
- Troop Regulations for appropriate ship as required?			
- Latest versions of MAGTF II/LOGAIS software loaded on computers?			
- FSSG Order P4030.1A, *SOP for PP&P*?			

ADMINISTRATION	YES	NO	N/A
Does the embarkation officer/assistant maintain an adequate turnover folder and desktop procedures?			
Does the embarkation officer's/assistant's desktop procedures contain, at a minimum, the following:			
- A list of pertinent orders and reference material?			
- POCs for embarkation (higher and lower echelon)?			
- A recall roster of embarkation personnel (higher and lower echelon)?			
- A current UDL of the unit's supplies and equipment?			
- Results of the last embarkation inspection?			
- A current list of supplies required for movement of the unit; e.g., NSN, nomenclature or cost?			
- Special sling requirements to lift the unit's equipment?			
- A list of required shoring/dunnage for air/sea movement?			
- A list of common hazards possessed by the unit?			
- A list of all key personnel within the unit that have received formal school training in TEO, HAZMAT, aircraft load planning, CSC, etc.?			
- A copy of unit box number allocations.			
- A copy of established procedures for requesting TOT and TOP?			
- A copy of established procedures for obtaining 463L pallets and nets?			
MDSS II			
Has the unit established and published procedures to update the garrison and/or the deployment UDLs?			
Does the unit embarkation officer/assistant conduct monthly evaluations/inspections on the maintenance of the garrison UDL?			
Does the UIC field reflect the correct UICs?			
Does the PKG_ID field reflect a correct box, pallet or serial of the item?			
Does the Item _ID field reflect the correct Item ID?			
Are descriptions in the UDL field sufficient for the commander to determine if the contents are required for an operation?			
Do the length, width, and height fields reflect the correct dimensional data?			
Does the JCS CCC field reflect the correct code for each item?			
Does the unit's garrison UDL accurately reflect all T/E, UER, individual material readiness list or other special allowance items?			
SUPPLIES			
Is sufficient lashing material available for cargo-carrying vehicles?			
Are there sufficient administrative supplies; e.g., tape, blank forms, and placards for embarkation?			
Are there sufficient wheel chalks with stringers for use during embarkation operations?			
Has the requirement for dunnage/shoring been identified for air movement of vehicles and equipment?			
Are there sufficient banding tools, clips, and 1 1/4- inch wire to band every container/box listed in the garrison UDL?			
Are there sufficient pallets with pallet boards for unbanded/unitized supplies and equipment listed in the garrison UDL?			
Does the unit have a supply of 463L pallet bags to protect cargo from the weather during an air movement?			
Does the embarkation officer/assistant have an architect scale, calculator, and tape measure?			

PREPARATION	YES	NO	N/A
Are boxes, vehicles, and containers marked IAW MARFORLANTO/MARFORPACO 4035.2/4035.1?			
Is there a box number placed on each box/container/pallet board or bundle?			
Are lifting devices installed on all vehicles and equipment?			
Are standard size boxes/containers being used to the maximum extent?			
PRESERVATION, PACKAGING, AND PACKING			
Does the unit have established procedures for requesting embarkation containers/boxes from PP&P?			
Does the unit maintain a PP&P log book?			
Does the unit have procedures to submit HAZMAT to PP&P for packaging and certification for shipment via surface or air?			
EMBARKATION SKILLS AND KNOWLEDGE EVALUATION			
Can the embarkation officer/assistant design and produce an ad hoc report given a specific format and criteria?			
Does the unit have a storage plan for supplies and left-behind equipment (LBE) that may be left behind due to limited lift capability?			
Does the embarkation officer/assistant understand the terms LBE and RBE?			
Can the embarkation officer/assistant demonstrate the procedures and considerations used during embarkation planning?			
Does the embarkation officer/assistant know what special MHE requirements they have?			
Can the embarkation officer/assistant explain a serial assignment table, landing sequence table, and assault table?			
Can the embarkation officer/assistant identify external transportation requirements to move their unit from origin to the POE?			
To what scale are sealift templates made?			
What is an SLCP?			
What is LFORM?			
What are the two types of loading for amphibious ships?			
Where would you find the capability of a specific class of amphibious ship?			
AIS PROFICIENCY			
Can unit embarkation personnel use the MDSS II Deployment Workbench function to source an accurate exercise or deployment UDL from MAGTF II?			
Can unit embarkation personnel use the MDSS II Workbench function to assign items scheduled to deploy with allocated air, surface or overland carriers?			
Can unit embarkation personnel create an MDSS II export for import to ICODES and AALPS?			
Can unit embarkation personnel use ICODES and AALPS to create templated loading plans as directed?			
Can unit embarkation personnel use AIT (LOGMARS, RFID) and MDSS II to enhance UDL management and provide ITV?			
REMARKS/RECOMMENDATIONS			

APPENDIX E
UNIT PERSONNEL AND TONNAGE TABLE LINE NUMBERS

The UP&TT line number helps personnel identify the contents in containers and select the best location to stow them aboard amphibious ships.

Embarkation personnel may select line numbers and mark them on the 3-inch diameter stowage designator on embarkation containers.

LINE NUMBER	ITEM
1	Rations
2	Water
3	Personal baggage (normally not used by unit embark NCO)
4	Organizational cargo (troop stow)
5	Organizational cargo (hold stow)
6	Construction/field fortification; e.g., cement, concertina wire or sandbags
7	Nonmilitary support (not normally carried in infantry units)
8	Medical and dental Items
9	Personal demand Items
10	Bulk fuel (more than 55 gal, not normally carried in infantry units)
11	Packaged fuel (55 gal or less, not normally carried in infantry units)
12	Chemicals (nonflammable); e.g., water purification material, water softening materials or fire extinguishing materials
13	Chemicals (flammable); e.g., gas cans, field lanterns, M-2 burners, white gas or immersion heaters
14	Compressed gas; e.g., oxygen or acetylene
15	Other POL (special lubes and greases); e.g., graphite, gear oil, instrument grease or wax
16	Small arm (.50 caliber and less small arms ammunition)
17	High explosives; e.g., artillery ammunition, demolition materials or hand grenades
18	Pyrotechnics; e.g., flares, thermites or blasting caps
19	Nuclear
20	Missiles
21	Inert; e.g., all training inert devices
22	Vehicles, equipment, heavy lifts; e.g., items that must require square foot stowage
23	Total square feet
24	Aircraft (operational)
25	Number of aircraft

APPENDIX F
RECOMMENDED EMBARKATION SUPPLIES AND EQUIPMENT

The following embarkation supplies and equipment should be available to the unit. As supplies are upgraded and different vendors are contracted to provide items, NSNs may change.

DESCRIPTION	NSN	TAMCN
BANDING MATERIAL/TOOLS		
Steel strapping, flat 1 1/4-inch	8135-00-283-0671	K4910
Seal, steel strapping (clip)	5340-00-891-3473	K4905
Sealer, steel strapping, hand (crimper)	5120-00-278-2423	K4806
Cutter	5110-00-223-6281	
Stretcher, steel strapping	3540-00-278-1250	K4948
LUMBER		
1 by 12 inches	5510-00-220-6086	
2 by 12 inches	5510-00-220-6202	
4 by 4 inches	5510-00-220-6226	
Plywood, 1/4-inch	5530-00-128-5419	
Plywood, 1/2-inch	5530-00-618-6958	
Plywood, 5/8-inch	5530-00-618-6959	
Plywood, 3/4-inch	5530-00-618-8073	
PACKAGING MATERIAL		
Adhesive, glue	various	
Bubble wrap	various	
Desiccant	various	
Foam rubber	various	
Paper, volatile corrosion inhibit	8135-00-664-4010	
Styrofoam	various	
Tape, masking	7510-01-242-6476	
Tape, pressure sensitive adhesive (duct)	7510-00-074-5124	K4975/K4980
PAINT MATERIAL		
Brush, paint 1-inch	8020-00-245-4508	
Brush, paint 2-inch	8020-00-245-4509	
Brush, paint 3 1/2-inch	8020-00-597-4777	
Roller kit, paint 7-inch	8020-00-597-4759	
Paint, black, spray	8010-00-582-5382	
Paint, Marine Corps green	8010-00-526-1607	
Paint, olive drab	8010-00-097-7901	
Paint, olive drab, spray	8010-00-141-2951	
Paint, red, spray	8010-00-721-9743	
Paint, white, spray	8010-00-584-3150	
Paint, yellow, spray	8110-00-141-2950	

DESCRIPTION	NSN	TAMCN
463L PALLET SYSTEM MATERIAL		
CGU-1, nylon strap, 5,000 lbs capacity (white)	1670-00-978-3851	
CGU-1, nylon strap, 5,000 lbs capacity (green)	5340-00-980-9270	
MB-1, tie-down chain, 10,000 lbs capacity	1670-00-516-8405	
MB-1, tensioning device, 10,000 lbs capacity	1670-00-212-1149	
Cover, plastic, pallet HCU-6/E	3990-00-930-1430	
Coupler, pallet (463L pallet)	1670-01-061-1990CT	
Coupler, pallet (KC-10)	1670-01-320-3637CT	
SCALES		
Scale, beam indicating platform type	300 lb capacity	C6000
Scale, beam indicating, platform type 1,000 lbs capacity		C6010
Scale, wheel-load, 20,000 lbs capacity		C4785
TOOLS		
Hammer, claw	5120-00-892-6263	
Saw, hand, crosscut	5110-00-142-4999	
Stencil, cutting, machine 1/2-inch	7490-00-164-0541	K4918
Stencil, cutting, machine 1-inch	7490-00-164-0537	C6280
Tape, measuring		
MISCELLANEOUS		
Rag, wiping	7920-00-205-1711	K4740
Rope, manila, 3 strands 1/2-inch	4020-00-231-2572	J3210
Stencil set 1/2-inch	7520-00-205-1760	
Stencil set 1-inch	7520-00-298-7043	
Stencil set 2-inch	7520-00-298-7044	
Stencil set 3-inch	7520-00-272-9683	
WATERPROOFING MATERIAL		
Barrier material (200 yds)	8135-00-282-0565	
Barrier material (200 yds)	8135-00-226-3124	
Adhesive, liquid (1 carton)	8040-00-273-8704	
Bag, plastic, 6 mil pallet box (50, 50 cu ft)	8105-00-191-3701	
Bag, plastic, gen purpose (50)	8105-01-174-0945	

Note: Plastic bags may be used in lieu of barrier paper and glue. If plastic bags are used, place one inside the box at all times.

The embarkation section should have the following typical supplies and equipment **prepacked** in an embarkation box or field desk for immediate use at a marshalling/staging area or at an APOE/SPOE. Quantities will vary based on historical usage data.

Note: the current wire banding material is being considered to be replaced by a nylon banding system.

DESCRIPTION	QTY	REMARKS
Nails		
Rope, 1/2-inch hemp or nylon		
Crimper, 1 1/4-inch		
Crimper, 3/4-inch		
Stretcher, 1 1/4-inch		
Banding cutter		
Banding wire 1 1/4-inch		
Banding wire 3/4-inch		
CGU-1 straps (5,000-lb)		
Pallet bags		
Hammer		
Screw drivers (assorted)		
Pliers		
Tape measure (50-foot)		
Knife		
Wheel scale		
Staple gun (heavy duty)		
Staples for staple gun		
PERSONAL SAFETY EQUIPMENT		
Safety helmet		
Gloves		
Goggles		
Safety vest		
Insect repellent		
Chem lights		
ADMINISTRATIVE SUPPORT ITEMS		
Baggage tags		
Tape (masking and duct)		
Clip board(s)		
Tablet (yellow/white)		
Paper clips		
Ruler		
Scale ruler		
Markers (black, red, green, blue) large		
Marker, waterproof (black)		
Placards (pallet and vehicle)		
Pens/pencils, with sharpener		
Folders		

ADMINISTRATIVE SUPPORT ITEMS		
DESCRIPTION	QTY	REMARKS
Envelopes (large and small)		
Stapler, regular w/staples		
White out/correction tape		
Dry markers w/eraser and clean fluid		
Post-its (large, medium, and small)		
Highlighter, various colors		
Work light (goose neck light)		
Plastic bags (large and small)		
Chalk (white and colored)		
Calculator (w/extra batteries)		
Calendar (current year)		
AMC PAM 36-1, *AMC Affiliation Program Airlift Planner's Guide*, and JP 3-02.2, *Joint Doctrine for Amphibious Embarkation*		
AIS COMPUTERS AND SUPPLIES		
Computer suite with printer		
Ship loading program and user's manual and ship's disk		
Aircraft loading program		
AIS program and user's manual		
HAZMAT/dangerous cargo program		
Computer paper		
Dangerous cargo forms, fan fold		
CDs/3.5-inch disks		
Extension cord (heavy duty)		
Surge protectors (bring two)		
Mouse pad		
Plotter		
Plotter ink cartridges		
Plotter paper		

APPENDIX G
OVERLAND TRANSPORTATION EQUIPMENT CAPABILITIES

TAMCN	MODEL	NOMENCLATURE	WEIGHT CAPACITY			CARGO LOADING AREA				
			XCOUNTRY (lbs)	HIGHWAY (lbs)	MAXIMUM PAX	LENGTH (in)	WIDTH (in)	HEIGHT (in)	FT2	FT 3
D0080	M353	3 1/2-ton TLR (generator)	7,000	8,000	N/A	109	49	—	37	—
D0198	MK23/25	7-ton truck, MTVR	15,000	30,000	18	168	88	96	103	582
D1059	M813	5-ton truck	10,000	20,000	18	168	88	68	103	582
D1059	M923	5-ton truck	10,000	20,000	18	168	88	68	103	582
D1061	M814	5-ton, extended bed	10,000	20,000	20	244	88	68	149	845
D1072	M817	5-ton dump truck	10,000	20,000	N/A	125	82	48	71	285
D0850	M101A2	3/4-ton TLR	1,500	1,500	N/A	76	65	68	35	195
D0860	M105A2	1 1/2-ton TLR	3,000	3,000	N/A	110	74	68	57	321
D0235	M870	40-ton low body TLR	80,000	80,000	N/A	216	96	96	144	1,152
D0876	MK14	Container haul TLR	25,000	45,000	N/A	239	96	96	160	1,275
D0879	MK17	Dropside cargo TLR	20,000	39,000	N/A	192	90	96	120	960
D0881	MK18	Ribbon bridge TLR	25,000	40,000	N/A	238	96	96	159	1,270
D1158	M998	HMMWV cargo variant	2,500	2,500	8	85	75	24	44	488
COMMERCIAL										
PAX		Bus	0	0	45	0	0	0	0	0
VEHICLES/CARGO										
		48-foot flatbed	0	42,000	0	576	96	96	384	3,072
		48-foot enclosed	0	42,000	0	576	96	96	384	3,072
		Drop deck	100,000		0	576	96	96	384	3,072
		Rail TLR	100,000		0					
		Low boy	80,000		0	204	96	96	136	
RAILCARS		DODX	300,000		0	1068	100		741	
		89-foot flat	100,000		0	1068	100		741	
		89-foot flat with side	100,000		0	1068	96		712	
		60-foot wooden deck	100,000		0	720	96		480	
		Container car	100,000		0	970	96		646	

APPENDIX H
TRANSPORTATION OF THINGS WORKSHEET

Submitted By: _____

| Name | Rank | Unit/Detachment | Phone | Date |

DET	PICKUP LOCATION BLDG #	PICKUP DATE	PICKUP TIME	POC	PHONE	CARGO	LxWxH	WEIGHT	DESTI-NATION	ARRIVE APOD		REMARKS
										DATE	TIME	

Note: POC—CWO2 in charge or SSgt Hardcorps, 725-6161.

APPENDIX I
TRANSPORTATION OF PEOPLE WORKSHEET

Submitted By: _____

Name _____ Rank _____ Unit/Detachment _____ Phone _____ Date _____

DET	PICKUP LOCATION	PAX PICKUP DATE	PAX PICKUP TIME	BAG PICKUP DATE	BAG PICKUP TIME	POC	PHONE	PAX COUNT	CARGO	DESTINATION	ARRIVAL TIME	FLIGHT TIME	REMARKS

Note: POC—CWO2 in charge or SSgt Hardcorps, 725-6161.

APPENDIX J
SAMPLE AMPHIBIOUS EMBARKATION
PREDEPLOYMENT MILESTONES

EVENT NUMBER	TARGET DATE	MILESTONES
1	Ongoing	MEU establishes early liaison with MSEs prior to operational control date.
2	Ongoing	MSEs conduct early liaison with planned attachments and produce UDL.
3	E-270	MEU determines assigned shipping from ESG.
4	E-270	MEU requests appropriate SLCPs/troop regs from ESG or other agencies.
5	E-270	Unit and TEOs assigned.
6	E-240	MEU conducts early embark liaison with ships.
7	E-230	MEU submits AMC channel request augmentees.
8	E-180	MSEs ensure all embarkation personnel are formal- school trained by this date.
9	E-180	MEU obtains LFORM data from each assigned ship.
10	E-180	MEU hosts logistics conference with MSEs and ESG.
11	E-180	MSEs provide complete UDL to MEU.
12	E-170	MEU develops landing plan.
13	E-160	MEU develops proposed initial assignment to shipping based on MEU commander's guidance, input from S-3, S-4, and MSEs.
14	E-160	MEU provides UDL to MEU service support group for procuring Class IX block.
15	E-160	Determine lift requirements and match against lift available.
16	E-150	MEU and MSEs order embarkation boxes as required; MSEs identify embarkation material deficiencies to MEU S-4.
17	E-140	ESG sends NSE augmentation message to MEU.
18	E-120	MEU and MSEs conduct preload conference with ESG.
19	E-60	ESG publishes LCAT.
*20	E-50	MEU submits OE&AS to the PHIBRON.
*21	E-45	Where required, ships submit pre-embarkation planning report to MEU.
*22	E-45	MEU submits staging area request to ESG.
*23	E-45	Final decisions on OE&AS are made; TEOs prepare message load plans (MLPs) as required.
*24	E-45	MSEs submit transportation, MHE, and convoy requirements to MEU.
*25	E-40	Where required, TEOs submit MLPs to MEU.
*26	E-30	MEU submits MLPs to ships as necessary.
*27	E-30	MEU submits training area request to CG, MCB Camp Pendleton (West Coast MEU).
*28	E-30	MEU submits consolidated transportation/MHE request to FSSG/LMCC; continues close coordination with FSSG.
*29	E-25	MEU publishes embarkation plan with tabs.
30	E-25	MEU conducts embarkation MSEs inspection.
*31	E-20	FSSG publishes movement schedule.
*32	E-15	Ships submit MLP response to MEU as required.
*33	E-15	ESG submits official BALS to MEU.

EVENT NUMBER	TARGET DATE	MILESTONES
*34	E-15	MEU/FSSG hosts final transportation planning conference with MSEs to discuss movement schedule.
*35	E-15	TEOs submit formal load plans to MEU to include final UDL.
*36	E-10	ESG hosts BALS conference.
*37	E-10	MEU submits formal load.
*38	E-5	Advance party/ship's platoon personnel to ships.
*39	E-DAY	Embarkation operations.
40	E+1.5	Ships submit EPMR to ESG.
41	E+2	COT submits LFORM/aviation ammunition mission load allowance inspection report to ESG.
42	E+5	COT prepares shipboard inspection summary for ship's captain's release.
* Indicates that this event occurs for any amphibious exercise.		

APPENDIX K
SAMPLE EMBARKATION PLAN

Copy no.__of__copies
CTF _/_ MEF (FWD)
PLACE OF ISSUE
Date/time group
Message reference number

TAB B (Embarkation Plan) to APPENDIX 14 (Amphibious Operations) to ANNEX C (Operations) (U)

(U) REFERENCES:

    (a) (S) CTF _/_ MEF Operation Order (OPORD) 1-99, UE 1-96
    (b) (S) PID 123_, JOPES Deployment Database
    (c) (U) DODR 4500.9-R, Parts I through IV
    (d) (U) JP 3-02.2
    (e) (U) FMFLantO P3120.15A, SOP for MAGTF Deployments
    (f) (U) IATA Dangerous Goods Regulations

TIME ZONE: Romeo

1. (U) Organization for Embarkation

    a. (U) General. II Marine expeditionary force (forward) (II MEF[FWD]) deploys via amphibious ships, AMC provided airlift, and transoceanic flight (self-deployable aircraft) to execute mission(s) detailed in reference (a) and redeploys to home stations/bases.

        (1) (U) II MEF(FWD) Deployment Organization

            II MEF(FWD)
              2d MARDIV(FWD)
              2d MAW(FWD)
              2D FSSG(FWD)

CLASSIFICATION

(2) (U) <u>Advance Party</u>. The advance party is limited to the liaison personnel required to coordinate initial support for II MEF forces at the designated advanced or intermediate staging bases (ISBs). The advance party element detailed in reference (b) will typically deploy to the designated advanced base or ISB via commercial airlift.

(3) (U) <u>Main Body</u>. The main body of II MEF(FWD) will deploy as indicated in reference (b) from Marine Corps Air Station (MCAS) Cherry Point, MCAS Beaufort, and the State Port at Morehead City. Mode of transportation will be flight ferry, AMC airlift, and amphibious shipping.

(4) (U) <u>Redeployment</u>. Redeployment of II MEF(FWD) forces will be accomplished using the same modes of transportation as used for the deployment. However, a rear party will be assigned to close out any advanced base/ISB concerns. The rear party will redeploy to home station/base via commercial airline service.

b. (U) <u>Assignment to Shipping</u>. Tab A to this OPORD provides the assignment to shipping. There has been no allocation of Military Sealift Command coordinated sealift for II MEF(FWD). Accordingly, all mission-essential personnel, supplies, and equipment must be airlifted to the ISB or loaded aboard amphibious sealift. Shortfalls in air or sealift have been reflected in reference (b).

2. (U) <u>Material to be Embarked</u>

a. (U) <u>Organic Equipment</u>. Allocation of AMC airlift and amphibious sealift is constrained so the following measures will be taken to ensure maximum use of assigned air and sealift.

(1) (U) <u>Mobile Loading</u>. All embarked vehicles/equipment will be mobile loaded to the maximum extent possible. Care must be taken to ensure mobile-loaded vehicles can fit into the designated vehicle stowage areas.

(2) (U) <u>Containerization</u>. Minimum bulk cargo space will be available to embarking units so all units will use PALCONs and QUADCONs and mobile load them to the maximum extent possible. In some cases these items will be exposed to the weather as they will be loaded on boat decks or helicopter landing spots.

(3) (U) <u>Vehicle Configuration</u>. Wherever possible all equipment dimensions will be reduced (length, width or height) to permit maximum use of available square foot stowage aboard shipping. However, the reduction in dimensions **must not** impact on that item's combat capability.

Page number

CLASSIFICATION

CLASSIFICATION

(4) (U) <u>Preloading of Landing Craft</u>. All landing craft utility (LCU) and landing craft air cushion (LCAC) will be preloaded with landing force equipment. Vehicles and equipment must be combat loaded (less weapons and ammunition) as there will be minimum capability to shift loads once embarked.

(5) (U) <u>463L Pallets</u>. Strategic airlift (STRATAIR) is limited so only items essential to the combat operations of II MEF will be deployed via STRATAIR. All 463L pallets will conform to the guidelines established in reference (c).

b. (U) <u>Types and Amounts of Supplies</u>

(1) (U) <u>Individual Combat Equipment (ICE)</u>. All II MEF forces will embark with their ICE stored in designated berthing spaces or mobile loaded in or on unit vehicles/equipment.

(2) (U) <u>Individual Weapons</u>. Individual weapons (M16A2, M9, M249) will be secured in rifle racks or in the designated armory spaces. All K-bars and bayonets will be stored in designated armory spaces.

(3) (U) All crew served and vehicle-mounted weapons will be stowed in the designated armory spaces.

(4) (U) Embarking units will not issue meals, ready to eat (MREs) to personnel prior to boarding ships. Required MREs will be issued prior to debarkation.

(5) (U) Embarking units will issue three MREs per person to personnel prior to arriving at the designated APOE. Meals will not be served onboard STRATAIR.

c. (U) <u>Preparation</u>

(1) (U) <u>Sealift</u>. Unit commanders and detachment OICs will ensure that all supplies and equipment are properly prepared for sealift per references (a), (d), (e), MSEs SOPs and the following:

(a) (U) All materials and equipment will be packaged to prevent physical damage, corrosion, deterioration, and water damage.

(b) (U) All supplies and equipment will be marked per reference (d) and this plan.

(c) (U) All embarkation boxes will be mobile loaded to the maximum extent possible to maximize use of landing force spaces.

Page number

CLASSIFICATION

CLASSIFICATION

(d) (U) All embarkation boxes not mobile loaded will be palletized to the maximum extent possible using 1 1/4-inch banding to secure boxes to the pallets. One-half inch banding may be used to secure individual embarkation boxes and PALCONs.

(e) (U) Waterproofing of vehicles and equipment will be IAW technical manuals. Minimal fixed port facilities are available for offload so plan for offload of all cargo and personnel via landing craft across the beach.

(f) (U) All vehicles embarked aboard amphibious shipping will have cargo compartment bows down and stowed. Canvas will be secured with mobile loaded cargo using 1/2-inch rope lashed in a zig-zag fashion. Tarps and canvas should not be placed over cargo as LCUs and LCACs will be used for ship-to-shore movement.

(g) (U) Vehicles and equipment to be loaded will be staged with not more than 3/4 tank of fuel.

(h) (U) All vehicles equipped to carry external fuel cans will carry full 5-gallon expeditionary cans. The following precautions will be taken when embarking vehicles with external fuel cans:

<u>1</u> Auxiliary fuel cans must comply with MCO P4030.19H.

<u>2</u> Inspect all fuel cans after filling to ensure that seals do not leak.

<u>3</u> Apply wire seals to fuel can cap to aid in detecting loosened caps or tampering.

<u>4</u> Motor gasoline will **not be embarked** without prior coordination with this command element and approval of the ship to be embarked.

<u>5</u> External fuel cans attached to vehicles will be filled to the top seal and wired shut. Vehicles may only carry as many fuel cans as there are external carriers (normally one per vehicle).

(i) (U) Drivers and assistant drivers will be designated by unit commanders and OICs for movement of vehicles and equipment from marshalling areas to the designated SPOE staging areas. Timeline for movement from marshalling area to SPOE staging areas will be issued by separate correspondence.

Page number

CLASSIFICATION

CLASSIFICATION

(j) (U) Hazardous cargo to be embarked aboard amphibious shipping will be identified to this command element via teleconference message in the II MEF (FWD) teleconference in the GCCS. All hazardous cargo will be segregated and labeled per CFR 49 and stowed separate from vehicles/equipment; e.g., gas cylinders, lithium batteries, corrosive, oxidizers or poisons. Oxygen and acetylene bottles on maintenance vehicles/equipment will be removed and properly packaged. A separate staging area will be available at the SPOE for hazardous cargo. Personnel delivering hazardous cargo to the port must report first to the II MEF(FWD) SLE to ensure that it is properly packaged and staged. Unit commanders and detachment OICs will ensure that hazardous cargo is **not** stored in vehicles, vans, QUADCONs, PALCONs or ISO containers during loading at unit areas.

(k) (U) Placards will be placed on all vehicles, equipment, vans, and containers (QUADCON and ISO). Placards will reflect the following information:

```
┌────────────────────────────────────────────────┐
│  UNIT LINE NUMBER: _____      │
│  SHIP: _____      │
│  VEHICLE TYPE: _____      │
│  HOLD/LEVEL: _____      │
│  DRIVER: _____      │
│  WEIGHT: _____      │
└────────────────────────────────────────────────┘
```

(l) (U) Placards will be placed as follows:

  1 Vehicles (inside windshield on **passenger** side and on driver's door).

  2 Trailers (driver's side and rear).

  3 ISO, QUADCON, and vans (one end and one side).

  4 Placards will be marked using a permanent pen/marker and protected from the elements by either a **clear** plastic bag or document protector.

(m) (U) It is imperative that total weights on placards are accurate, especially for ISOs, QUADCONs, and vans as these items will be picked up using forklifts or cranes.

Page number

CLASSIFICATION

CLASSIFICATION

(2) (U) <u>Airlift</u>. Unit commanders and detachment OICs will ensure that all supplies and equipment are prepared for STRATAIR per references (c), (e), (f), MSEs SOP, and as follows:

(a) (U) All materials and equipment will be packaged to afford maximum protection against physical and material handling damage, corrosion, deterioration, and water damage.

(b) (U) All supplies and equipment will be marked per references (c) and (f).

(c) (U) All embarkation boxes will be secured to warehouse pallets to the maximum extent possible using 1 1/4-inch banding. One-half inch banding may be used to secure individual embarkation boxes and PALCONs.

(d) (U) Cargo mobile loaded in vehicles will be loaded no higher than the wooden sideboards or the metal side of the cargo compartment of the vehicle. All vehicles will have cargo compartment bows down and stowed. Canvas will be secured with mobile loaded cargo using 1/2-inch rope lashed in a zig-zag fashion. Mobile loaded cargo can not exceed cross country-weight rating of vehicle.

(e) (U) Vehicles and equipment will be staged with not more than 3/4 tank of fuel for vehicles to be loaded on aircraft cargo floor or 1/2 tank for ramp loaded vehicles.

(f) (U) All vehicles equipped to carry external fuel cans will carry full 5-gallon expeditionary cans. The following precautions will be taken when embarking vehicles with external fuel cans:

<u>1</u> Expeditionary fuel cans must comply with Military Specification MIL-C-1283E, *Auxiliary Fuel Cans*.

<u>2</u> Inspect all fuel cans after filling to ensure that seals do not leak.

<u>3</u> External fuel cans attached to vehicles will be filled to the top seal and wired shut. Vehicles may only carry the number of fuel cans that equals two full-fuel tanks.

(g) (U) Drivers and assistant drivers will be designated by unit commanders and OICs for movement of vehicles and equipment from marshalling areas to the designated APOE staging areas. Timeline for movement from marshalling area to APOE staging areas will be issued by separate correspondence.

(h) (U) All vehicles and equipment will arrive at the designated APOE not later than 24 hours **prior** to the scheduled arrival of the assigned mission.

Page number

CLASSIFICATION

CLASSIFICATION

(i) (U) All vehicles will be weighed and marked with the front axle, rear axle, combined weight, and center of balance at unit marshalling areas (prior to departing for APOE). Unit commanders and detachment OICs will ensure **no additional** cargo is placed on or in vehicles once weighing is completed.

(j) (U) 463L cargo pallets will arrive at the designated APOE weighed, marked, and netted 24 hours prior to scheduled arrival of the assigned mission. This includes classified cargo. Departing units will coordinate security requirements with the II MEF airlift liaison element (ALE).

(k) (U) Baggage pallets, if required, will be built at the APOE by the embarking unit under ALE supervision. All baggage must arrive at the APOE with the personnel, 3 hours prior to scheduled departure.

(l) (U) Hazardous cargo to be deployed aboard AMC airlift will be identified to this command element via teleconference message in the II MEF(FWD) teleconference available in GCCS. All hazardous cargo will be segregated, packaged, certified, and labeled per DODR 4500.9-R, Part II and MCO P4030.19H. A separate staging area will be available at the APOE for hazardous cargo. Personnel delivering hazardous cargo to the APOE must report first to the II MEF(FWD) ALE to ensure that it is properly packaged and staged. Unit commanders and detachment OICs will ensure that hazardous cargo stored in vehicles, vans, QUADCONs, PALCONs or ISO containers is properly identified prior to departing origin.

(m) (U) Unit commanders and detachment OICs will ensure that vehicles, containers, vans, and locked shelters are accompanied by a unit representative with a set of keys for inspection by the DACG and II MEF(FWD) ALE. **If keys are not available at the time of joint inspection, the locks will be cut.**

(n) (U) Placards will be placed on all vehicles, equipment, vans, 463L pallets, and containers (QUADCON and ISO) and contain the following information:

```
UNIT LINE NUMBER:_____

VEHICLE TYPE: _____

DRIVER/UNIT: _____

WEIGHT:_____

L" x W" x H":_____
```

Page number

CLASSIFICATION

CLASSIFICATION

(o) (U) Placards will be placed as follows:

1 Vehicles. Inside windshield on passenger side and on driver's door.

2 Trailers. Driver's side and rear.

3 463L pallets, ISO, QUADCON, and vans. One end and one side.

4 Placards will be marked with a permanent pen/marker and protected from the elements by using a **clear** plastic bag or a document protector.

(p) (U) It is imperative that total weights on placards are accurate. Weights must include all mobile loaded cargo.

d. (U) <u>Marshalling, Movement, and Staging</u>. Marshalling and movement are the responsibility of unit commanders and detachment OICs. All movement from origin to SPOE/APOE will be accomplished in strict compliance with reference (e). II MEF (FWD) movement schedule will be the single document used to phase all personnel, supplies, and equipment from origin to POE.

(1) (U) <u>Sealift</u>. Specific information for marshalling and staging in support of deployment by amphibious shipping.

(a) (U) MSEs will are responsible for all aspects of unit preparation and marshalling at the origin to include vehicles and equipment are properly prepared for embarkation.

(b) (U) MSEs will review all movement schedules to ensure preparation and marshalling are completed prior to movement to the staging areas. Any delays or problems beyond the unit's ability to correct will be reported to the parent UMCC in an expeditious manner for resolution.

(c) (U) TEOs and unit representatives will monitor the arrival and staging of unit supplies and equipment at the SPOE to ensure they are staged in the proper areas and are accounted for. Any vehicles or equipment not arriving at the SPOE in a timely manner will be reported to the II MEF SLE expeditiously. The SLE will contact the LMCC, for coordination with route patrol, to attempt to locate the missing vehicles/equipment.

(d) (U) MSEs will provide drivers/working parties (under the direction of a staff NCO (SNCO) or officer with a working knowledge of how to properly prepare cargo/vehicles for sealift movement) at the SPOE to assist the SLE in loading and or correcting discrepancies.

CLASSIFICATION

CLASSIFICATION

(2) (U) <u>Airlift</u>. Specific information for the marshalling and staging in support of deployment by AMC or commercial airlift.

(a) (U) MSEs will ensure close supervision of all aspects of unit preparation and marshalling at the origin. Ensuring all preparations conform to standards already addressed.

(b) (U) MSEs will review all movement schedules to ensure completion of preparation and marshalling prior to movement to the staging areas. Any delays or problems beyond the unit's ability to correct will be reported to the parent UMCC in an expeditious manner for resolution.

(c) (U) MSEs will ensure that all vehicles and 463L cargo pallets arrive at the APOE not later than 24 hours prior to scheduled arrival of assigned mission.

(d) (U) MSEs will ensure personnel arrive, with their baggage, at the designated APOE not later than 3 hours prior to scheduled departure of assigned mission. The assigned plane team commanders will ensure all personnel assigned to their mission are manifested and in the designated holding area not later than 2 hours prior to scheduled departure time.

(e) (U) Deploying units will provide initial aircraft load plans to the II MEF (FWD) ALE prior to staging. Upon completion of staging and JI the unit will update the initial aircraft load plan and provide the II MEF(FWD) ALE with a completed copy of the load plan.

(f) (U) MSEs will provide working parties (under the SNCO's direction or officer with a working knowledge of how to properly prepare cargo/vehicles for air movement) at the APOE to correct any discrepancies that arise after staging has been completed and during the JI process.

(g) (U) MSEs that have a classified cargo requirement or will embark with security ammunition will notify the II MEF(FWD) ALE at least 24 hours prior to arrival at APOE to ensure an appropriate cargo storage area is available.

(h) (U) Passenger manifesting will take place at Building 4210, MCAS Cherry Point. II MEF (FWD) G-1, augmented by each MSE, will coordinate flight manifests for each mission. Each MSC is responsible for providing detailed personnel listing and databases to II MEF(FWD).

Page number

CLASSIFICATION

CLASSIFICATION

e. (U) <u>Movement</u>. Movement of II MEF(FWD) forces will be accomplished in strict compliance with reference (e). IAW reference (e), CG, II MEF will activate the deployment support organizations required to assist in the control and coordination of the deployment of forces.

(1) (U) II MEF(FWD) will activate the MAGTF movement control center (MCC) on release of this document. On order, elements of II MEF(FWD) will activate a UMCC and provide the location, telephone number and, if available, facsimile (FAX) number to the MAGTF MCC. MAGTF MCC is located in Wing 1B (North), Building H-1. MCC information is as follows:

Telephone Numbers: Primary: Defense Switched Network (DSN)
                                              484-8492
                  Secondary: DSN 484-8497
                  Commercial: (910) 451-XXXX
                  FAX: DSN 484-8397

(2) (U) The MAGTF MCC will consolidate all II MEF(FWD) transportation requirements and resolve any conflicts by prioritizing them prior to providing them to the LMCC. All changes to movement requirements will be forwarded to the MCC.

(3) (U) II MEF(FWD) will provide a consolidated movement schedule detailing the movement of all organic assets to the APOE/SPOE based on the arrival schedule of strategic transportation. Adjustments to this schedule should be anticipated due to shifting of supported commanders requirements.

(4) (U) Commencing 24 hours prior to movement to APOE/SPOE the MAGTF MCC will conduct an initial movement coordination meeting with all deploying element representatives. Following, a daily coordination meeting will be held with all element representatives to review the **next** 24 to 72 hours of movement.

(5) (U) MSEs are authorized direct liaison with the LMCC to expedite the development of movement plans; however, all movement plans will be coordinated through II MEF(FWD).

CLASSIFICATION

CLASSIFICATION

3. (U) <u>Personnel</u>

    a. (U) <u>Uniform, Equipment, and Baggage</u>. The uniform for deployment of all II MEF (FWD) forces is camouflage utilities for personnel deploying aboard amphibious shipping or AMC/commercial aircraft. Personnel deploying helicopters or fixed-wing aircraft will deploy in appropriate flight gear. A detailed uniform and equipment list has been provided by II MEF (FWD) G-1 in separate correspondence. All personnel will deploy with their individual weapon and are limited to one seabag or Val-pack/ suitcase, one all-purpose lightweight individual carrying equipment (ALICE) pack, and one hand-carry bag. Total weight allocation for baggage and combat equipment is 120 pounds (175 for aircrew). This weight restriction is critical for PAX deploying via AMC or commercial airlift.

    b. (U) <u>Advance Parties and Ship's Platoons</u>

        (1) (U) <u>Advance Parties</u>. There will be limited advance parties authorized for the deployment of II MEF (FWD) forces. All advance party requirements will be coordinated via II MEF (FWD) G-3 and G-1.

        (2) (U) <u>Ship's Platoons</u>. Each ship's platoon to be embarked aboard amphibious ships is typically required to arrive at their designated ship **no earlier/later than** 48/24 hours prior to sailing. Ship's platoon will deploy with all personal and military equipment. Ship's platoons will depart from origin via commercial contracted bus. Ship's platoon OIC will report to the CCO or first lieutenant (1st LT). The COT or his designated representative and the billeting officer for the embarking force will also deploy with the ship's platoon. COT will make the required advance liaison with the ship's executive officer while the billeting officer initiates joint inventory of landing force spaces. Ship's platoon will include the following personnel:

        (3) (U) <u>Cooks, Bakers, and Mess Men</u>. Number of these personnel per ship will be coordinated by the COT per the SLCP.

        (4) (U) <u>Laundry Detail</u>. Number per each SLCP.

        (5) (U) <u>Ships Store</u>. Number per each SLCP.

        (6) (U) <u>Guides</u>. Number of guides per ship will vary. Details will be coordinated by the COT with the CCO or ship's 1stLT.

CLASSIFICATION

CLASSIFICATION

(7) (U) <u>Combat Cargo Personnel</u>. These personnel will work directly for the ship's CCO or the combat cargo assistant (CCA). These personnel will be split between the flight and well deck for operations. The number of personnel will vary per ship. Designated COT for each ship will coordinate with the CCO/CCA for number of personnel required.

(8) (U) <u>Guard Force</u>. Total guard force will be coordinated by the COT with the CCO or ship's 1stLT. This force consists of, at a minimum the following:

    (a) (U) One guard officer.

    (b) (U) Two sergeants of the guard.

    (c) (U) Two corporals of the guard.

    (d) (U) Sentries (four per post). Posts are designated in each ship's SLCP.

c. (U) <u>Movement of Main Bodies</u>

(1) (U) Movement of the II MEF(FWD) main body by sealift is detailed in reference (b). All movement of personnel will be closely monitored by the MAGTF MCC, LMCC, and the SLE to ensure no bottlenecks occurs to affect the onload of personnel at the SPOE. The main body will be embarking at various points. Each unit will be designated a specific location for embarkation, based on the II MEF (FWD) movement plan. Locations include but are not limited to the following:

    (a) (U) State port at Morehead City.

    (b) (U) Radio Island (adjacent to the state port facility).

    (c) (U) Onslow Beach (vicinity of Risley Pier).

    (d) (U) MCAS New River (helicopter squadron fly-on).

(2) (U) Movement of the II MEF(FWD) main body by airlift is detailed in reference (b). All movement of personnel will be closely monitored by the MAGTF MCC, LMCC, and the ALE to ensure no bottleneck occurs that may affect the throughput of personnel at the APOE. The main body will be embarking at various points. Each unit will be designated a specific location for embarkation, based on the II MEF (FWD) movement plan. II MEF (FWD) main body personnel deploying via airlift will deploy from the following locations:

    (a) (U) MCAS Cherry Point.

    (b) (U) MCAS Beaufort.

Page number

CLASSIFICATION

CLASSIFICATION

d. (U) <u>Embarkation Rosters and Passenger Manifests</u>. All rosters for embarking II MEF (FWD) forces will be developed and issued using the current logistics and administrative AIS. II MEF (FWD) G-1 has issued specific guidance as to format and required data elements. Five copies of each ship's embark roster will be provided to the designated COT. One of these copies will be provided to the CCO or ship's 1stLT. For airlift, ten copies of the passenger manifests will be provided to the designated plane team commander. One additional copy will be provided to the DACG OIC and one copy to the ALE OIC. Eight copies will be provided to the aircrew and the other two copies will be retained by the plane team commander for the APOD presentation.

4. (U) <u>Embarkation Areas</u>

a. (U) <u>Assignment of Areas and Embarkation Points</u>. II MEF(FWD) forces will deploy from various locations in and around the MCB Camp Lejeune, MCAS Beaufort, and MCAS Cherry Point area. Specific embarkation areas and points are provided in TAB C of this plan.

b. (U) <u>Preparation</u>. The LMCC is responsible for ensuring the proper preparation of the designated embarkation areas and points detailed in TAB C.

c. (U) <u>MHE</u>. MHE at all embarkation areas is under the direct control of the LMCC through the:

    (1) (U) POG.

    (2) (U) BOG.

    (3) (U) DACG.

Any augmentation requirements will be identified by the LMCC and coordinated by the II MEF FMCC. Crane support at the state port will be identified to the II MEF(FWD) MCC for further ID to the LMCC.

d. (U) <u>Security and Counterintelligence</u>. The security of all USMC property is the responsibility of all personnel. The following are specific security arrangements for the II MEF(FWD) deployment.

    (1) (U) <u>March Routes</u>. Civilian authorities in coordination with the military police of Camp Lejeune and MCAS Cherry Point will patrol the primary march route to the designated APOE and SPOE. The LMCC will establish checkpoints at the critical chokepoints en route to the APOE and SPOE. The checkpoints and military police will use the same radio frequency. Coordination with civilian authorities will be via commercial telephones.

Page number

CLASSIFICATION

CLASSIFICATION

(2) (U) <u>Marshalling Areas</u>. MSEs are responsible for establishing and maintaining security of their designated marshalling areas. The LMCC will coordinate with the military police at MCB Camp Lejeune, MCAS New River, MCAS Cherry Point, and MCAS Beaufort for a roving patrol to be established to cover the designated unit marshalling areas.

(3) (U) <u>Staging Areas and Embarkation Points</u>

(a) (U) <u>MCAS Cherry Point.</u> The MCAS Cherry Point military police will establish a checkpoint at the vehicle entrance to the APOE. No privately owned vehicles will be permitted within the confines of the APOE. The DACG will establish a badge and escort system for vehicle control. All personnel assigned to DACG, ALE or TALCE are required to wear a security badge at all times. All other personnel must be escorted when outside of Building 4209 (DACG headquarters). The II MEF(FWD) will establish a roving guard within the confines of the APOE from nondeploying personnel. This guard force will report to the II MEF(FWD) OIC ALE. MSEs will not provide an independent guard force for their equipment.

(b) (U) <u>MCAS Beaufort</u>. The MCAS Beaufort military police will establish checkpoints at the designated staging areas for Marine Aircraft Group-31 (MAG-31) and Marine Wing Support Squadron-273. All personnel entering these areas must be on an access roster or possess a security badge issued by the military police. MAG-31 has been directed to provide a roving patrol to provide continuous monitoring of the staging area.

(c) (U) <u>State Port at Morehead City</u>. The port has civilian guards at the gates leading into the port facility that will be augmented by military police. All personnel entering the port facility, not part of a military convoy, must be identified on an access roster. Access rosters will be coordinated by the LMCC. II MEF(FWD) will establish an internal guard force to patrol the designated staging areas. This guard force will be under the control of the SLE and consist of nondeploying personnel.

(d) (U) <u>Embarkation Points at Onslow Beach</u>. Units designated to embark personnel and equipment/vehicles via LCAC and LCU from Onslow Beach will provide security for those items from the time they are staged for loading until they have departed the beach for the ship. These guard personnel will be in radio communication with the parent command at all times.

Page number

CLASSIFICATION

CLASSIFICATION

(4) (U) <u>Counterintelligence</u>. All unauthorized entries will be reported immediately to the MAGTF MCC. All questions from civilians or news paper/media personnel will be forwarded to the II MEF public affairs office representative. All personnel apprehended in security areas will be detained for interview by civilian and military police.

5. (U) <u>Embarkation Schedules</u>

    a. (U) <u>Limiting Dates</u>

        (1) (U) <u>Marshalling</u>. Marshalling of II MEF(FWD) supplies and equipment will commence upon receipt of the warning order. Movement from marshalling areas is **not authorized** unless directed by II MEF(FWD) MCC.

        (2) (U) <u>Movement to APOE/SPOE</u>. Movement from the marshalling areas to the designated APOE/SPOE will commence when directed by CG II MEF(FWD). The movement will be in strict compliance with the MAGTF movement schedule. All movement will be controlled and coordinated via the LMCC.

        (3) (U) <u>Movement from APOE/SPOE</u>. The strategic leg of the deployment will be per the schedules contained in JOPES. The JOPES database contains the key dates for availability of forces at the designated APOE/SPOE.

    b. (U) <u>Loading Schedules</u>

        (1) (U) <u>Amphibious Shipping</u>. Tab D contains the detailed berthing and loading schedules for II MEF(FWD) amphibious shipping.

        (2) (U) <u>Airlift Schedules</u>. Airlift schedules are contained in reference (b). These schedules are distributed to all MSEs at the daily coordination meeting. The MAGTF movement schedule for airlifted forces will be adjusted, as required, to conform with airflow.

6. (U) <u>Control</u>

    a. (U) <u>Traffic Circulation and Control</u>

        (1) (U) <u>March Routes</u>. The primary and secondary march routes to the APOE and SPOE will be designated by the II MEF(FWD) motor transport officer in conjunction with the LMCC. Strip maps of the routes with checkpoints will be issued to all convoy commanders by the II MEF(FWD) MCC.

Page number

CLASSIFICATION

CLASSIFICATION

(2) (U) All convoys will obey the traffic regulations posted on march routes. Speed of convoys will not exceed 45 mph or the posted limits (whichever is less).

(3) (U) Only the II MEF(FWD) MCC is authorized to release tactical vehicle convoys from their marshalling areas. The MAGTF MCC will report the release of each convoy to the LMCC. The II MEF(FWD) SLE/ALE located at the designated SPOE and APOE will report the arrival of each convoy to the II MEF(FWD) MCC.

(4) (U) Vehicle movement within the SPOE and APOE will be strictly controlled, as these areas will be extremely congested. Specific traffic patterns will be established and enforced in the vicinity, and within the APOE and SPOE. These traffic patterns will be fully briefed by the LMCC to each MSE moving equipment through these POEs.

(5) (U) <u>Movement of Personnel</u>. Excluding drivers and assistant drivers, the majority of personnel deploying via strategic airlift and amphibious shipping will travel to the POE via commercial contracted busses. All busses will be coordinated by the LMCC based on the MAGTF movement schedule. All requested changes to the movement schedule will be coordinated through the MAGTF MCC.

b. (U) <u>Embarkation Liaison Elements</u>. II MEF(FWD) will establish embarkation liaison elements at the designated APOEs and SPOEs.

(1) (U) <u>Sealift</u>. A SLE will be established at the State Port of Morehead City. The SLE will be collocated with the POG. The SLE will be activated 24 hours prior to the movement of any supplies or equipment to the port.

(2) (U) <u>Airlift</u>. An ALE will be established at MCAS Cherry Point APOE facility. The ALE will be collocated with the DACG. The ALE will be activated and in place not later than 48 hours prior to the scheduled arrival of the first aircraft.

(3) (U) <u>Movement Control</u>

(a) (U) <u>MAGTF</u>. II MEF (Fwd) will establish a MAGTF MCC. The MAGTF MCC is located in Building H-1, Wing 1B (North), MCB Camp Lejeune. The MCC is the single coordination point for all movements.

Page number

CLASSIFICATION

CLASSIFICATION

(b) (U) <u>II MEF</u>. CG, II MEF will activate the FMCC to support the deployment efforts of II MEF (FWD). The FMCC exercises control over the deployment of all forces in support of II MEF(FWD) and based on the MAGTF commander's concept of deployment. CG, II MEF will direct the activation of deployment support organizations to assist in the deployment efforts of the MAGTF. The LMCC is the MEF commanders single point of coordination and control for deployment and deployment support. The LMCC will orchestrate all activities necessary to support the marshalling, movement, staging, and loading of II MEF(FWD) forces. Detailed information on the activities and responsibilities can be found in reference (e).

(c) (U) <u>Communications</u>. Primary means of communications between embarkation control offices will be via telephone. Communications in the marshalling areas, and staging areas will be via hand-held radios. All hand-held radios will have two frequencies: MAGTF MCC and LMCC. The MAGTF MCC, ALE, SLE, DACG, POG, and LMCC are also linked together via local/wide area network. All route checkpoints will be linked to the LMCC using tactical radio frequencies established by the LMCC and II MEF. Additional hand-held frequencies or tactical radio frequencies will be added as required to control and coordinate movement.

7. (U) <u>Miscellaneous</u>

   a. (U) <u>Loading Plans</u>

(1) (U) <u>Amphibious Shipping</u>. TEOs will prepare combat load plans for their designated ship using the ICODES. TEOs will provide the II MEF(FWD) SLE with a diskette containing the UDL file used to develop the ICODES load plans prior to sailing from SPOE. Completed load plans will include all standard documentation required by joint, multi-Service or Marine Corps doctrinal guidance.

(a) (U) Once reviewed and signed by the CO of the ship, the TEO will ensure the ship is loaded per the approved load plan. The CCO or ship's 1stLT must coordinate any proposed deviations from the approved load plan.

(b) (U) Upon completion of loading, the TEO will ensure any approved changes to the load plan are made in ICODES and a corrected copy is provided to the ship and two copies are provided to the II MEF(FWD) SLE.

CLASSIFICATION

(2) (U) <u>AMC Airlift</u>. All C-130, C-141B, C-17, C-5B, and KC-10 load plans will be developed in the AALPS. All units deploying via AMC airlift will provide the ALE with a copy of the load planning database and one copy of the load plan at the time of staging. Databases/load plans will be adjusted to reflect the actual item dimensions and weights validated during the JI.

b. (U) <u>Loading Reports</u>. Loading and actual departure reports for surface and airlift movement is forwarded to higher headquarters through two channels with different data requirements for each. The FMCC receives reports from the LMCC, POG, BOG and DACG on the status of loading and on actual departure times. While the MAGTF MCC receives reports from the MAGTF liaison to the LMCC, ALE, and SLE. The ALE and SLE provides detailed information on the amount of tonnage and numbers of PAX departing on each ship and aircraft. The FMCC has established specific reporting criteria in reference (e) while the specific reporting criteria and formats for the ALE, and SLE are contained in appendix 4 of reference (a).

c. (U) <u>Database Reconciliation</u>. The deployment database (JOPES) must be updated by II MEF as the units depart to provide visibility of closure of deploying forces and to accurately reflect the numbers of personnel and amounts of supplies and equipment deployed. In doing this, the MAGTF MCC includes personnel to track and update the progress of the deployment. II MEF elements must thoroughly and continuously review their deployment data to ensure it reflects the actual requirements of the unit. The deployment database will be used by the MAGTF MCC to continue to allocate lift assets to obtain force closure.

CLASSIFICATION

APPENDIX L
WESTPAC EXPRESS

The WESTPAC Express is an HSV modified to support movement of III MEF forces from Okinawa and MCAS Iwakuni, Japan throughout the WESTPAC region.

Loading Cargo and Vehicles on the Car Deck

Embarkation personnel have eight lanes on mezzanine decks to load cargo and vehicles on the car deck.

Two mezzanine decks can each stow 12 low-back HMMWVs or equivalent in a row, with a maximum height of 74 inches. The height reduction for low-back HMMWVs can be quickly achieved by disconnecting the fording gear exhaust extension from the chassis and rotating the assembly aft. The maximum allowable single axle weight on the mezzanine decks is 3,500 pounds.

Two under mezzanine decks can stow up to 13 high-back HMMWVs or equivalent in a row. The minimum overhead clearance is 108 inches; the maximum allowable single axle weight is 4,500 pounds.

The port and starboard main decks each have two lanes to stow helicopters, heavy wheeled and tracked vehicles, and cargo. For ease and speed of loading and discharge, heavy vehicles and helicopters are typically stowed on the port and starboard outboard lanes. The inboard lanes, port and starboard of the centerline stanchions, are used to stow QUADCONs and 463L pallets loaded with bulk cargo and baggage. The maximum allowable single axle weight for these decks is 26,455 pounds; the maximum allowable dual axle weight is 33,069 pounds. The maximum

allowable individual vehicle is 88,184 pounds; the minimum overhead clearance is 180 inches.

The port and starboard main deck outboard lanes each have a length of 2,484 feet available to stow heavy vehicles, such as the medium tactical vehicle replacement, AAVs, LAVs, LVSs, and helicopters.

The port-side inboard lane is located directly aft of a refrigerated 20-foot ISO container. This container stows unit rations that will be consumed while underway, and has 167 feet of deck space available to stow QUADCONs and 463L pallets. Sufficient space for access to the refrigerated container has already been factored-in.

The starboard inboard lane is located directly aft of the ship's lube oil drum storage area and has 196 feet available for QUADCON and 463L pallet stowage.

Miscellaneous

The ship has no means of moving fuel or other liquids from port to starboard to balance the vessel's trim. Always ensure the overall starboard side vehicle and cargo load is 30,000 to 50,000 pounds heavier than the port side load.

The vessel's optimum bow down attitude, which ensures the smoothest ride possible for embarked personnel and best speed and fuel economy, is between 20 centimeters and 1 meter. The ship can move fuel from the forward tanks to the aft tanks but is time consuming. The best technique to achieve the optimum bow down attitude is to load the lightest vehicles in the forward area of the mezzanine and main vehicle decks, with vehicle weights increasing until the heaviest vehicles are placed in the vicinity of the stern ramp.

See table L-1 on page L-2 for general characteristics.

Table L-1. WESTPAC Express Characteristics.

Length	101 meters
Beam	26.65 meters
Gross tonnage	8,403 metric tons
Speed (operational)	30-32 knots
Speed (maximum)	40 knots
Draft at maximum cargo load	4.5 - 4.8 meters
Crew	14 (13 civilian mariners and 1 USMC operations officer)
PAX	970
Cargo	531 short tons (at maximum fuel load; the payload can be increased, if necessary, by reducing fuel levels)
Ramp	1 stern
Main engines	4 Caterpillar™ 3618 diesels
Propulsion	4 Kamewa™ 125 SII waterjets
Range	At maximum cargo load, maximum fuel load and a speed of 32 knots: 1,344 nautical miles.
Design	Twin hull Catamaran™
Builder	Austal Ships of Henderson, Western Australia
Date launched	09 April 2001
Date delivered to III MEF	11 July 2001

APPENDIX M
GLOSSARY

Section I. Acronyms and Abbreviations

AACG . . . . arrival airfield control group
AALPS . . . . .automated air load planning system
AAV . . . . amphibious assault vehicle
AAVP . . . .amphibious assault vehicle, personnel
AB. . . . . .air base
ACA . . . . .airlift clearance authority
AC/S . . . . .assistant chief of staff
ADP . . . . .automated data processing
AFB . . . . Air Force Base
AFR. . . . . Air Force Regulation
AIS . . . . .automated information system
AIT . . . . . . automated identification technology
ALD . . . . .available-to-load date
ALE. . . . . .airlift liaison element
ALICE. . . . . . .all-purpose lightweight individual
carrying equipment
AMC . . . . Air Mobility Command
AMCPAM. . . . Air Mobility Command Pamphlet
AMovP . . . . Allied Movement Publication
AO . . . . .area of operations
APERS . . . . authorized personnel
APOD . . . . .aerial port of debarkation
APOE . . . . aerial port of embarkation
AR. . . . . .Army regulation
ATF . . . . amphibious task force

BALS . . . . berthing and loading schedule
BUMEDINST . . . . .Bureau of Medicine and
Surgery instruction

C2 . . . . .command and control
CAM . . . . commercial air movement
CATF . . . . . .commander, amphibious task force
CCA . . . . combat cargo assistant
CCC . . . . cargo category code
CCO . . . . combat cargo officer
CD. . . . . compact disk
C-day. . . . . .commencement day
CE . . . . command element
CFR . . . . Code of Federal Regulations

CG . . . . commanding general
CGRI . . . . .commanding general's
readiness inspection
CJCSM . . . . Chairman of the
Joint Chiefs of Staff manual
CLF . . . . commander, landing force
CO .commanding officer
COMMARFORLANT . . . . Commander, Marine
Corps Forces, Atlantic
COMMARFORPAC . . . . . Commander, Marine
Corps Forces, Pacific
COMNAVSURFLANT . . . . Commander, Naval
Surface Force, Atlantic
COMNAVSURFLANTINST . . . . . .Commander,
Naval Surface Force,
Atlantic instruction
COMNAVSURFPAC. . . . . . Commander, Naval
Surface Force, Pacific
COMNAVSURFPACINST . . . . . . .Commander,
Naval Surface Force,
Pacific instruction
CONOPS . . . . .concept of operations
CONUS . . . . .continental United States
COT . . . . commanding officer of troops
CSC . . . . .International Convention of
Safe Containers
CSSE . . . . .combat service support element
CTF. . . . . .combined task force
CTUS . . . . customs territory of the US
CU. . . . . .cubic
CWO . . . . .chief warrant officer

DACG . . . . .departure airfield control group
DD . . . . Department of Defense
Dest. . . . . destination
DET . . . . .detachment
DOD . . . . Department of Defense
DODR. . . . . . .Department of Defense regulation
DODX . . . . Department of Defense-owned
railcars

DR . . . . .dual role
DSN . . . . .Defense Switched Network
DTR . . . . . . .Defense Transportation Regulation
DTS . . . . .Defense Transportation System

EAD . . . . .earliest arrival date
E-day . . . . embarkation day
e-mail. . . . . electronic mail
EPMR . . embarked personnel and material report
ESG. . . . . .expeditionary strike group
EWTGPAC . . . . Expeditionary Warfare
Training Command Pacific

FAX . . . . .facsimile
FDP&E . . . . force deployment planning
and execution
FFCC. . . . . .flight ferry control center
FMCC . . . . force movement control center
FMFLantO. . . . . .Fleet Marine Force
Atlantic Order
FRAG . . . . fragmentation code
FRN. . . . . force requirement number
FSSG. . . . . force service support group
ft . . . . foot/feet
ft2 . . . . square foot
ft3 . . . . .cubic foot
FW. . . . . fixed wing
FWD . . . . .forward
FY . . . . .fiscal year

G-1. . . . . .general staff administration section
G-3 . . . . general staff operations section
G-4 . . . . .general staff logistics section
G-5. . . . . general staff plans section
gal . . . . .gallon
GBL . . . . government bill of lading
GCCS . . . Global Command and Control System
GEOCODE . . . . .geographic code
GSORTS . . . . .global status of resources
and training system

HALFCON . . . . .half container
HAZMAT . . . . .hazardous materials
HHQ . . . . higher headquarters
HMMWV . . . . high mobility
multipurpose
wheeled vehicle
HQ. . . . . .headquarters
HQMC. . . . . Headquarters, Marine Corps
hr . . . . hour

hrs . . . . hours
HSV .high speed vessel

IATA . . International Air Transport Association
IAW .in accordance with
ICAO. . . . . .International Civil Aviation
Organization
ICE . . . . individual combat equipment
ICODES . . . . integrated computerized
deployment system
ID . . . . identification
IMDG . . . . . . .International Maritime Dangerous
Goods
IMO. . . . . . .International Maritime Organization
in . . . . inch
INSERT . . . . insert code
ISB . . . . .intermediate staging base
ISO . . . . International Organization for
Standardization
ITS . . . . individual training standards
ITV . . . . in-transit visibility

J-4 . . . . Joint staff logistics directorate
JA/ATT . . . . joint airborne/joint transportability
training
JCS .Joint Chiefs of Staff
JFAST . . . . . . .joint flow and analysis system for
transportation
JHSV . . . . .joint high speed vessel
JI . . . . joint inspection
JOPES . . . . Joint Operation Planning and
Execution System
JP . . . . .joint publication
JTF . . . . .joint task force

LAD . . . . latest arrival date
LARC-V . . . . lighter, amphibious, resupply,
cargo 5-ton
LAV . . . . .light armored vehicle
LBE. . . . . left-behind equipment
lb . . . . .pound
LCAC . . . . landing craft air cushion
LCAT . . . . .landing craft availability table
LCU . . . . landing craft, utility
LDO . . . . limited duty officer
LF . . . . landing force
LFORM . . . . .landing force operational
reserve material
LHA. . . . . amphibious assault ship-general
purpose

LHD . . . . .amphibious assault ship-multipurpose
LMCC . . . . .logistic and movement
control center
LOGAIS . . . . . . .logistics automated information
system
LOGMARS . . . . logistics applications of
automated marking
and reading symbols
LOI .letter of instruction
LPD . . . . .amphibious transport dock
LRA . . . . logistics readiness assessment
LRI . . . . .logistics readiness inspection
LSD . . . . .dock landing ship
LT . . . . lieutenant
LtCol. . . . . .lieutenant colonel
LVS . . . . .Logistics Vehicle System

M1A1 . . . . .Abrams tank
MAG. . . . . .Marine aircraft group
MAGTF . . . . Marine air-ground task force
Maj . . . . major
MARDIV . . . . Marine division
MARFOR . . . . .Marine Corps forces
MARFORLANT. .Marine Corps Forces, Atlantic
MARFORLANTO . . . . . . .Marine Corps Forces,
Atlantic order
MARFORPAC . . . .Marine Corps Forces, Pacific
MARFORPACO . . . . .Marine Corps Forces,
Pacific order
MAW . . . . Marine aircraft wing
MCAS. . . . . .Marine Corps air station
MCB . . . . Marine Corps base
MCC . . . . movement control center
MCCSSS . . . . Marine Corps Combat
Service Support Schools
MCI . . . . Marine Corps Institute
MCIP . . . .Military Customs Inspection Program
MCO . . . . Marine Corps order
MCRP . . . . .Marine Corps reference publication
MCWP . . .Marine Corps warfighting publication
MDSS II . . . . Marine air-ground task force
Deployment Support System II
MEF . . . . Marine expeditionary force
MEF(FWD). . . . . Marine expeditionary force
(forward)
MEU . . . . Marine expeditionary unit
MHE . . . . materials handling equipment
MIL-HDBK . . . . military handbook

MILSTAMP . . . .military standard transportation
and movement procedures
M/L . . . . .manning level
MLP . . . . message load plan
mm . . . . .millimeter
MOS . . . . . military occupational specialty
MOT . . . . .mission-oriented training
MPF . . . . maritime prepositioning force
mph. . . . . miles per hour
MPS . . . . maritime prepositioning ships
MPSRON . . . . maritime prepositioning ships
squadron
MRE . . . . .meal, ready to eat
MSC . . . . major subordinate command
MSE . . . . .major subordinate element
MTMC . . . . .Military Traffic Management
Command (now Surface
Deployment and Distribution
Command
MTMCTEA . . . . . .Military Traffic Management
Command Transportation
Engineering Agency
MTON . . . . measurement ton
MTT . . . . mobile training team
MTVR . . . .medium tactical vehicle replacement
MV . . . . .motor vessel

N/A . . . . .not applicable
NAS . . . . naval air station
NATO . . . . . .North Atlantic Treaty Organization
NAVMC . . . . Navy Marine Corps
NBC . . . . .nuclear, biological, and chemical
NCO . . . . .noncommissioned officer
N-day . . . . .notification for deployment day
NMWP . . . . . . Nonmanufactured Wood Packing
NRPAX. . . . . .number passengers
NS . . . . .naval station
NSDA . . . . non-self deployment aircraft
NSE . . . . Navy support element
NSN . . . . National Stock Number
NVG .night vision goggle

OCCFLD . . . . .occupational field
OE&AS. . . . . . organization for embarkation and
assignment to shipping
OIC . . . . officer in charge
OPLAN . . . . .operation plan
OPORD. . . . . .operation order

OSA . . . . .operational support airlift
PALCON . . . . palletized container
PAM . . . . .pamphlet
PAX . . . . passengers
PCS . . . . number of pieces - quantity
PEI . . . . principal end item
PHIBRON . . . . .amphibious squadron
PIC . . . . parent indicator code
PID . . . . plan identification
PKGID . . . . package identification
PME . . . . professional military education
PMT . . . . preventive medicine technician
POC. . . . . point of contact
POD . . . . .port of debarkation
POE . . . . port of embarkation
POG . . . . .port operations group
POL . . . . .petroleum, oils, and lubricants
PP&P . . . . preservation, packaging, and packing
psi . . . . .pounds per square inch
PTC . . . . plane team commander

QTY . . . . quantity
QUADCON . . . . quadruple container

RAT . . . . .readiness assessment team
RBE . . . . remain-behind equipment
RDD . . . . required delivery date
regs . . . . regulations
RFID . . . . radio frequency identification
RLD . . . . ready-to-load date
ROG . . . . .railhead operations group
RO/RO . . . . roll-on/roll-off
RW . . . . .rotary-wing

S-1 . . . . staff administration section
S-2 . . . . staff intelligence section
S-3 . . . . staff operations section
S-4 . . . . staff logistics section
S-6 . . . . .staff communications section
SAAM. . . . . . . special assignment airlift mission
SAV . . . . staff assistance visit
SDDC . . . . Surface Deployment and Distribution
Command (formerly
Military Traffic Management
Command)
SECNAVINST . . . . .Secretary of the Navy
instruction

SIXCON . . . . six containers together
SLCP. . . . . .ship's loading characteristics
pamphlet
SLE . . . . sealift liaison element
SMO . . . . strategic mobility officer
SNCO . . . . .staff noncommissioned officer
SOP . . . . standing operating procedures
SPOD . . . . seaport of debarkation
SPOE. . . . . .seaport of embarkation
SRC. . . . . .source
SS . . . . .steam ship
STANAG . . . . standardization agreement
(NATO)
S/T . . . . short ton
STRATAIR. . . . . strategic airlift
SVC. . . . . service code

TACC . . . . .tanker airlift control center
TACLOG . . . . tactical-logistical
TAD . . . . temporary additional duty
T-AK. . . . . container and roll-on/roll-off ship
TALCE . . . . tanker airlift control element
TAMCN . . . . table of authorized materiel
control number
TCC . . . . .transportation component commander
TCN . . . . transportation control number
T/E . . . . table of equipment
TEO . . . . .team embarkation officer
TLR. . . . . trailer
TM . . . . technical manual
TMO . . . . transportation management office
T/O . . . . table of organization
TOP. . . . . transportation of people
TOT. . . . . transportation of things
TPFDD . . . . time-phased force and
deployment data
TRK . . . . .truck
TUCHA . . . . type unit characteristics
TWCF . . . . .Transportation Working
Capital Fund

UDL . . . . unit deployment list
UER . . . . .unit equipment report
UIC . . . . unit identification code
ULN .unit line number
UMCC . . . . unit movement control center
UP&TT . . . . . . unit personnel and tonnage table

US .... United States
USAF .... United States Air Force
USCS .... United States Customs Service
USDA .... United States Department
of Agriculture
USMC .... United States Marine Corps
USN .... United States Navy
USNS .... United States Naval Ship
USS .... United States Ship

USTRANSCOM .... United States
Transportation Command
UTC .... unit type code

vol .... volume

WESTPAC .... Western Pacific

yd .... yard

Section II. Terms

aerial port—An airfield that has been designated for the sustained air movement of personnel and materiel as well as an authorized port for entrance into or departure from the country where located. (JP 1-02)

aerial port of debarkation—A station which serves as an authorized port to process and clear aircraft and traffic for entrance to the country in which located.

aerial port of embarkation—A station which serves as an authorized port to process and clear aircraft and traffic for departure to the country in which located.

airhead—**1.** A designated area in a hostile or threatened territory which, when seized and held, ensures the continuous air landing of troops and materiel and provides the maneuver space necessary for projected operations. Normally it is the area seized in the assault phase of an airborne operation. **2.** A designated location in an area of operations used as a base for supply and evacuation by air. (JP 1-02)

Air Mobility Command—The Air Force component command of the US Transportation Command. Also called **AMC**. (JP 1-02)

allowable cabin load—The maximum payload that can be carried on an individual sortie. Also called **ACL**. (JP 1-02)

automated air load planning system—An automated system to select, sequence, and prioritize aircraft load plans.

available-to-load date—A date specified for each unit in the time-phased force and deployment data indicating when that unit will be ready to load at the port of embarkation. Also called **ALD**. (JP 1-02)

bulk—Cargo that fits within the usable dimensions of a 463L pallet (84 x 104 inches).

C-day—The unnamed day on which a deployment operation commences or is to commence. The deployment may be movement of troops, cargo, weapon systems, or a combination of these elements using any or all types of transport. The letter "C" will be the only one used to denote the above. The highest command or headquarters responsible for coordinating the planning will specify the exact meaning of C-day within the aforementioned definition. The command or headquarters directly responsible for the execution of the operation, if other than the one coordinating the planning, will do so in light of the meaning specified by the highest command or headquarters coordinating the planning.

cargo—Supplies, materials, stores, baggage, or equipment transported by land, water, or air. **a. bulk. dry or liquid cargo**—(oil, coal, grain, ore, sulfur, or fertilizer) that is shipped unpackaged in large quantities. Also, air cargo that fits within the dimensions of a 463L pallet and the design height of 96 ft. **b. containerizeable cargo**—Items that can be stowed or stuffed into a container closed military container moved via ocean (SEAVAN) or military vans (containers) (MILVANs) (i.e., overdimensional or overweight cargo). **c. noncontainerizeable cargo**—Items which cannot be stowed or stuffed into SEAVANs or MILVANs (i.e., overdimensional or overweight cargo). **d. oversize**—Air cargo that exceeds the dimensions of bulk cargo but is equal to or less than 1,090 ft in length, 117 ft in width, and 105 ft in height. **e. outsize**—Air cargo that exceeds the dimensions of oversize cargo and requires the use of a C-5 or C-17 aircraft. **f. source stuffed cargo**—Cargo that economically fills a container from a single point of origin.

carrier—Any individual, company, or corporation commercially engaged in transporting cargo, passengers, or household goods.

channel airlift—Common-user airlift service provided on a scheduled basis between two points. There are two types of channel airlift. A requirements channel serves two or more points on a scheduled basis depending upon the volume of traffic; a frequency channel is time-based and serves two or more points at regular intervals. (JP 1-02)

closure—In transportation, the process of a unit arriving at a specified location. It begins when the first element arrives at a designated location, e.g., port of entry and/or port of departure, intermediate stops, or final destination, and ends when the last element does likewise. For the purposes of studies and command post exercises, a unit is considered essentially closed after 95 percent of its movement requirements for personnel and equipment are completed. (JP 1-02)

common-user lift—US Transportation Command-controlled lift. The pool of strategic transportation assets either government-owned or chartered that are under the operational control of Air Mobility Command, Military Sealift Command, or Surface Deployment and Distribution Command for the purpose of providing common-user transportation to the Department of Defense across the range of military operations. These assets range from common-user assets available day-to-day to a larger pool of common-user asset phased in from other sources.

contingency plan—A plan for major contingencies that can reasonably be anticipated in the principle geographic subareas of the command. (JP 1-02)

Defense Transportation System—That portion of the Nation's transportation infrastructure which supports Department of Defense common-user transportation needs across the range of military operations. It consists of those common-user military and commercial assets, services, and systems organic to, contracted for, or controlled by the Department of Defense. Also called **DTS**. (JP 1-02)

deliberate planning—**1.** The Joint Operation Planning and Execution System process involving the development of joint operation plans for contingencies identified in joint strategic planning documents. Deliberate planning is accomplished in prescribed cycles that complement other Department of Defense planning cycles in accordance with the formally established Joint Strategic Planning System. **2.** A planning process for the deployment and employment of apportioned forces and resources that occurs in response to a hypothetical situation. Deliberate planners rely heavily on assumptions regarding the circumstances that will exist when the plan is executed. (JP 1-02)

depositioning—A mission to return the aircraft from bases at which missions have terminated.

detailed planning—The Joint Operations Planning and Execution System function that includes both the deliberate planning phases of plan development, plan review, and supporting plans and the crisis action planning phase of execution planning.

dual role—Any mission where both air refueling and airlift are provided to the user.

earliest arrival date—A day relative to C-day, that is specified by a planner as the earliest date when a unit, a resupply shipment, or replacement personnel can be accepted at a port of debarkation during a deployment. Used with the latest arrival data, it defines a delivery window for transportation planning. Also called **EAD**. (JP 1-02)

execution planning—The phase of the Joint Operation Planning and Execution System crisis action planning process that provides for the translation of an approved course of action into an executable plan of action through the preparation of a complete operation plan or operation order. Execution planning is detailed planning for the commitment of specified forces and resources. During crisis action planning, an approved operation plan or other President and/or Secretary of Defense-approved course of action is adjusted, refined, and translated into an operation order. Execution planning can proceed on the basis of prior deliberate planning, or it can take place in the absence of prior planning.

frustrated cargo—Any shipment of supplies and/or equipment which, while en route to destination, is stopped prior to receipt and for which further disposition instructions must be obtained. (JP 1-02)

government bill of lading—A government document used to procure transportation and related services from commercial carriers.

intermodal—Type of international freight system that permits transshipping among sea, highway, rail and air modes of transportation through use of American National Standards Institute/International Organization for Standardization standard containers, line-haul assets and handling equipment. (JP 1-02)

International Civil Aviation Organization (Code)—Four-letter codes that identify a country by the first letter and an airfield by the last three letters. (All continental United States codes begin with "K.")

in-transit visibility—The ability to track the identity, status, and location of Department of Defense units, and non-unit cargo (excluding bulk petroleum, oil, and lubricants) and passengers; patients; and personal property from origin to consignee or destination across the range of military operations. Also called **ITV**. (JP 1-02)

intratheater—Within a theater. (JP 1-02)

joint—Connotes activities, operations, organizations, etc., in which elements of two or more Military Departments participate. (JP 1-02)

joint airborne/air transportability training—A Chairman of the Joint Chiefs of Staff-directed, Air Mobility Command-managed program to provide basic airborne and proficiency/continuation training for airdrop, assault airland, and aircraft static loading conducted in a joint environment.

Joint Operation Planning and Execution System—A system that provides the foundation for conventional command and control by national- and combatant command-level commanders and their staffs. It is designed to satisfy their information needs in the conduct of joint planning and operations. Joint Operation Planning and Execution System (JOPES) includes joint operation planning policies, procedures, and reporting structures supported by communications and automated data processing systems. JOPES is used to monitor, plan, and execute mobilization, deployment, employment, sustainment, and redeployment activities associated with joint operations. Also called **JOPES**. (JP 1-02)

joint task force—A joint force that is constituted and so designated by the Secretary of Defense, a combatant commander, a subunified commander, or an existing joint task force commander. Also called **JTF**. (JP 1-02)

level of detail—Within the current joint planning and execution systems, movement characteristics are described at five distinct levels of detail. **a. level I**-aggregated level—Expressed as total number of passengers and total short tons, total measurement tons, total square feet, and/or total hundreds of barrels by unit line number (ULN), cargo increment number (CIN), and personnel increment number (PIN). **b. level II**-summary level—Expressed as total number of passengers by ULN and PIN and short tons, measurement tons (including barrels), total square feet of bulk, oversize, outsize, and non-air-transportable cargo by ULN and CIN. **c. level III**—detail by cargo category—Expressed as total number of passengers by ULN and PIN and short tons and/or measurement tons (including barrels) as well as total square feet of cargo as identified by the ULN or CIN three-position cargo category code. **d. level IV**—detail expressed as number of passengers and individual dimensional data (expressed in length, width, and height in number of inches) of cargo by equipment type by ULN. **e. level V**—detail by priority of shipment—Expressed as total number of passengers by Service specialty code in deployment sequence by ULN, individual weight (in pounds), and dimensional data (expressed in length, width, and height in number of inches) of equipment in deployment sequence by ULN. **f. level VI**—Detail expressed for passengers by name and social security number or for coalition forces and civilians by country national identification number; and for cargo by transportation control number (TCN). Nonunit cargo includes Federal Stock Number/National Stock Number detail. Cargo can be nested. Cargo with TCNs that are nested are referred to as "secondary load". Example: 11 vehicles of the same type would be represented by 11 level VI records. These records would be summed to I in level IV record. (JP 1-02)

measurement ton—The unit of volumetric measurement of equipment associated with surface delivered cargo. Measurement tons equal total cubic feet divided by 40 (1MTON = 40 cubic feet). Also called **M/T, MT, MTON.** (JP 1-02)

mobility—A quality or capability of military forces which permits them to move from place to place while retaining the ability to fulfill their primary mission. (JP 1-02)

mobilization—1. The act of assembling and organizing national resources to support national objectives in time of war or other emergencies. **2.** The process by which the Armed Forces or part of them are brought to a state of readiness for war or other national emergency. This includes activating all or part of the Reserve Components as well as assembling and organizing personnel, supplies, and materiel. Mobilization of the Armed Forces includes but is not limited to the following categories. **a. selective mobilization**—Expansion of the active Armed Forces resulting from action by Congress and/or the President to mobilize Reserve Component units, Individual Ready Reservists, and the resources needed for their support to meet the requirements of a domestic emergency that is not the result of an enemy attack. **b. partial mobilization**—Expansion of the active Armed Forces resulting from action by Congress (up to full mobilization) or by the President (not more than 1,000,000 for not more than 24 consecutive months) to mobilize Ready Reserve Component units, individual reservists, and the resources needed for their support to meet the requirements of a war or other national emergency involving an external threat to the national security. **c. full mobilization**—Expansion of the active Armed Forces resulting from action by Congress and the President to mobilize all Reserve Component units in the existing approved force structure, as well as all individual reservists, retired military personnel, and the resources needed for their support to meet the requirements of a war or other national emergency involving an external threat to the national security. Reserve personnel can be placed on active duty for the duration of the emergency plus six months. **d. total mobilization**—Expansion of the active Armed Forces resulting from action by Congress and the President to organize and/or generate additional units or personnel beyond the existing force structure, and the resources needed for their support, to meet the total requirements of a war or other national emergency involving an external threat to the national security. (JP 1-02)

non-unit-related cargo—All equipment and supplies requiring transportation to an operational area, other than those identified as the equipment or accompanying supplies of a specific unit. (e.g., resupply, military support for allies, and support for nonmilitary programs, such as civil relief). (JP 1-02)

operational control—Command authority that may be exercised by commanders at any echelon at or below the level of combatant command. Operational control is inherent in combatant command (command authority) and may be delegated within the command. When forces are transferred between combatant commands, the command relationship the gaining commander will exercise (and the losing commander will relinquish) over these forces must be specified by the Secretary of Defense. Operational control is the authority to perform those functions of command over subordinate forces involving organizing and employing commands and forces, assigning tasks, designing objectives, and giving authoritative direction necessary to accomplish the mission. Operational control includes authoritative direction over all aspects of military operations and joint training necessary to accomplish missions assigned to that command. Operational control should be exercised through the commanders of subordinate organizations. Normally this authority is exercised through subordinate joint force commanders and Service and/or functional component commanders. Operational control normally provides full authority to organize commands and forces and to employ those forces as the commander in operational control considers necessary to accomplish assigned missions; it does not, in and of itself, include authoritative direction for logistics or matters of administration, discipline, internal organization, or unit training. Also called **OPCON**. (JP 1-02)

operation plan—Any plan, except for the Single Integrated Operational Plan, for the conduct of military operations. Plans are prepared by combatant commanders in response to requirements established by the Chairman of the Joint Chiefs of Staff and by commanders of subordinate commands in response to requirements tasked by the establishing unified commander. Operation plans are prepared in either a complete format (OPLAN) or as a concept plan (CONPLAN). The CONPLAN can be published with or without a timephased force and deployment data (TPFDD) file. **a. OPLAN**—An operation plan for the conduct of joint operations that can be used as a basis for development of an operation order (OPORD). An OPLAN identifies the forces and supplies required to execute the combatant commander's strategic concept and a movement schedule of these resources to the theater of operations. The forces and supplies are identified in TPFDD files. OPLANs will include all phases of the tasked operation. The plan is prepared with the appropriate annexes, appendixes, and TPFDD files as described in the Joint Operation Planning and Execution System manuals containing planning policies, procedures, and formats. Also called **OPLAN. b. CONPLAN**—An operation plan in an abbreviated format that would require considerable expansion or alteration to convert it into an OPLAN or OPORD. A CONPLAN contains the combatant commander's strategic concept and those annexes and appendixes deemed necessary by the combatant commander to complete planning. Generally, detailed support requirements are not calculated and TPFDD files are not prepared. **c. CONPLAN with TPFDD**—A CONPLAN with TPFDD is the same as a CONPLAN except that it requires more detailed planning for phased deployment of forces. Also called **CONPLAN**. (JP 1-02)

opportune lift (air)—The use of organic aircraft in a secondary role to the primary mission and the portion of airlift capability available to common user traffic for use after planned mission requirements have been used. Opportune airlift is a by-product of positioning, depositioning and training missions, and will not degrade or interfere with the primary/planned mission.

opportune lift (sea)—Space available cargo. Will not interfere with the primary/planned mission.

outsized cargo—Cargo which exceeds the dimensions of oversized cargo and requires the use of a C-5 or C-17 aircraft or surface transportation. A single item that exceeds 1,000 inches long by 117 inches wide by 105 inches high in any one dimension. See also **oversized cargo**. (JP 1-02)

oversized cargo—Air cargo exceeding the usable dimension of a 463L pallet loaded to the design height of 96 inches, but equal to or less than 1,000 inches in length, 117 inches in width, and 105 inches in height. This cargo is air transportable on the C-5, C-17, C-141, C-130, KC-10 and most civilian contract cargo carriers. See also **outsized cargo**. (JP 1-02)

port of debarkation—The geographic point at which cargo or personnel are discharged. This may be a seaport or aerial port of debarkation; for unit requirements; it may or may not coincide with the destination. Also called **POD**. (JP 1-02)

port of embarkation—The geographic point in a routing scheme from which cargo or personnel depart. This may be a seaport or aerial port from which personnel and equipment flow to a port of debarkation; for unit and nonunit requirements, it may or may not coincide with the origin. Also called **POE**. (JP 1-02)

positioning—Mission performed to relocate aircraft for the purpose of conducting a mission.

Ready Reserve Fleet—United States Government-owned fleet of commercially designed deep-draft ships of various configurations and capabilities maintained by the Maritime Administration to respond within four, five, ten or twenty days to

national emergency sealift requirements, particularly the movement of military unit equipment.

SIXCON—A module unit, which consists of five water or fuel tank modules and one pump module. The SIXCON modules attach together to form a 20-foot equivalent unit (ISO container). The modules form a liquid distribution source that can be transported as a unit or quickly taken apart for rapid deployment or relocation.

strategic air—The airlift capability necessary to deploy and sustain military forces worldwide in support of national strategy. Also called **STRATAIR**.

strategic lift—Air, land, and sea transport assets designated for deploying forces and cargo between theaters of operations or between the continental United States and theaters of operations.

strategic mobility—The capability to deploy and sustain military forces worldwide in support of national strategy. (JP 1-02)

strategic sealift—The afloat prepositioning and ocean movement of military materiel in support of US and multinational forces. Sealift forces include organic and commercially acquired shipping and shipping services, including chartered foreign-flag vessels and associated shipping services. (JP 1-02)

supported commander—**1.** The commander having primary responsibility for all aspects of a task assigned by the Joint Strategic Capabilities Plan or other joint operation planning authority. In the context of joint operation planning, this term refers to the commander who prepares operation plans and operation orders in response to requirements of the Chairman of the Joint Chiefs of Staff. **2.** In the context of a support command relationship, the commander who receives assistance from another commander's force or capabilities, and who is responsible for ensuring that the supporting commander understands the assistance required. (JP 1-02)

supporting commander—1. A commander who provides augmentation forces or other support to a supported commander or who develops a supporting plan. Includes the designated combatant commands and Defense agencies as appropriate. **2.** In the context of a support command relationship, the commander who aids, protects, complements, or sustains another commander's force, and who is responsible for providing the assistance required by the supported commander. (JP 1-02)

sustainment—The provision of personnel, logistic, and other support required to maintain and prolong operations or combat until successful accomplishment or revision of the mission or of the national objective. (JP 1-02)

theater—The geographical area outside the continental United States for which a commander of a combatant command has been assigned responsibility. (JP 1-02)

time-phased force and deployment data—The Joint Operation Planning and Execution System database portion of an operation plan; it contains time-phased force data, non-unit-related cargo and personnel data, and movement data for the operation plan, including the following: **a.** In-place units; **b.** Units to be deployed to support the operation plan with a priority indicating the desired sequence for their arrival at the port of debarkation; **c.** Routing of forces to be deployed; **d.** Movement data associated with deploying forces; **e.** Estimates of non-unit-related cargo and personnel movements to be conducted concurrently with the deployment of forces; and **f.** Esti-

mate of transportation requirements that must be fulfilled by common-user lift resources as well as those requirements that can be fulfilled by assigned or attached transportation resources. Also called **TPFDD**. (JP 1-02)

ton—A measurement of weight: long ton equals 2,240 pounds, measurement ton equals 40 cubic feet, metric ton equals 2,204.6 pounds, and short ton equals 2,000 pounds.

unified command—A command with a broad and continuing mission under a single commander and composed of significant assigned components of two or more Military Departments that is established and so designated by the President through the Secretary of Defense with the advice and assistance of the Chairman of the Joint Chiefs of Staff.

validate—Execution procedure used by combatant command components, supporting combatant commanders, and providing organizations to confirm to the supported commander and US Transportation Command that all the information records in a time-phased force and deployment data not only are error free for automation purposes, but also accurately reflect the current status, attributes, and availability of units and requirements. Unit readiness, movement dates, passengers, and cargo details should be confirmed with the unit before validation occurs. (JP 1-02)

war reserve materiel—That portion of materiel, above and beyond peacetime operating stocks, required to support the increase activity of forces during wartime. War reserve materiel is necessary to assure the timely response and sustainability of weapon systems to support forces, activities and mission objectives for wartime scenarios. Also called WRM.

APPENDIX N
REFERENCES

Code of Federal Regulations (CFRs)

Title 46   Shipping
Title 49   Transportation

Department of Defense Directive (DODD)

5030.49   DOD Customs and Border Clearance Program

Department of Defense Regulation (DODR)

4500.9-R   Defense Transportation Regulation
                Part I, Passenger Movement
                Part II, Cargo Movement
                Part III, Mobility
                Part V, DOD Customs and Border Clearance Policies
                   and Procedures
                Part VI, Management and Control of Intermodal
                   Containers and System 463-L Equipment

North Atlantic Treaty Organization (NATO) Publications

STANAG 2236   Multimodal Movement and Transport Matters
STANAG 2454   Regulations and Procedures for Road Movements and
                   Identification of Movement Control and Traffic Control
                   Procedures and Agencies
AMovP-01A   Regulations and Procedures for Road Movements and
                   Identification of Movement Control and Traffic Control
                   Procedures and Agencies
AMovP-5   Multimodal Transport Issues

Chairman of the Joint Chiefs of Staff Manuals (CJCSMs)

3122.01   Joint Operation Planning and Execution System (JOPES),
               Volume I (Planning, Policies, and Procedures)
3122.02C   Joint Operation Planning and Execution System (JOPES),
               Volume III (Crisis Action Time-Phased Force and
               Deployment Data Development and Deployment
               Execution)
3122.03A   Joint Operation Planning and Execution System (JOPES),
               Volume II, Planning Formats and Guidance

Joint Publications (JPs)

1-02	Department of Defense Dictionary of Military and Associated Terms
3-02	Joint Doctrine for Amphibious Operations
3-02.2	Joint Doctrine for Amphibious Embarkation
4-01.2	Joint Tactics, Techniques, and Procedures for Sealift Support to Joint Operations
4-01.3	Joint Tactics, Techniques, and Procedures for Movement Control
4-01.5	Joint Tactics, Techniques, and Procedures for Transportation Terminal Operations
4-01.6	Joint Tactics, Techniques, and Procedures for Joint Logistics Over-the-Shore (JLOTS)
4-01.7	Joint Tactics, Techniques, and Procedures for Use of Intermodal Containers in Joint Operations
4-01.8	Joint Tactics, Techniques, and Procedures for Joint Reception, Staging, Onward Movement, and Integration
4-07	Joint Tactics, Techniques, and Procedures for Common User Logistics During Joint Operations

Naval Warfare Publications (NWPs)

4-01.1	Navy Expeditionary Shore-Based Logistics Support and Reception, Staging, Onward Movement and Integration (RSOI) Operations
4-04.1	SEABEE Operations in the MAGTF

Marine Corps Warfighting Publications (MCWPs)

3-31.5	Ship-to-Shore Movement
3-32	Maritime Prepositioning Force Operations
4-11	Tactical-Level Logistics
4-11.3	Transportation Operations
4-11.8	Services in an Expeditionary Environment
4-12	Operational-Level Logistics
5-1	Marine Corps Planning Process

Marine Corps Reference Publications (MCRPs)

3-31B	Amphibious Ships and Landing Craft Data Book
4-11C	Combat Cargo Operations Handbook
5-12D	Organization of Marine Corps Forces

Secretary of the Navy Instructions (SECNAVINSTs)

5510.30A   Department of the Navy Personnel Security Program

6210.2A/   Quarantine Regulations of the Armed Forces
AR 40-12/
AFR 161-4

Bureau of Medicine and Surgery Instruction (BUMEDINST)

6250.12C   Pesticide Applicator Training and Certification for Medical
                              Personnel

Marine Corps Orders (MCOs)

1510.61C   Individual Training Standards (ITS) System for
                              Embarkation/Logistics Occupational Field 04

P4000.51A   Automatic Identification Technology Policy Manual

P4030.19H   Preparing Hazardous Materials for Military Air Shipments

4631.10A   Operational Support Airlift Management

Marine Corps Technical Manual (TM)

11240-15/4C   Motor Transport Technical Characteristics Manual

Commander Naval Surface Forces Atlantic/Commander Naval Surface Forces Pacific Instruction (COMNAVSURFLANTINST/COMNAVSURFPACINST)

9010.2/9010.1   Ship's Loading Characteristics Pamphlet (SLCP)

COMNAVSURFLANTINST (East Coast Commands Only)

3000.3   Landing Force Spaces and Material Aboard
                              COMNAVSURFLANT Ships

COMNAVSURFPACINSTs (West Coast/WESTPAC Commands Only)

4621.1A   Standard Amphibious Embarkation Documentation Procedures

7320.1   Troop Space Inventory/Inspection/Reimbursement Procedures

Marine Corps Forces Atlantic Order (MARFORLANTO)/Marine Corps Forces, Pacific Order (MARFORPACO)

4035.2/4035.1   Tactical Marking Procedures for Equipment and Embarkation
                              Containers

Miscellaneous

AFR 76-11, US Government Rate Tariffs

AMC PAM 36-1, AMC Affiliation Program Airlift Planner's Guide

Aviation Logistics Support Ship T-AVB Logistics Planning Manual

Charters-Special Assignment Airlift Missions (SAAMs), Joint Chiefs of Staff Exercises (JCSE), and Contingencies for the Transportation Working Capital Fund (TWCF), and Non-TWCF Aircraft Civil Air Mobility Command Pamphlet (AMCP) 55-41, Civil Reserve Air Fleet (CRAF) Load Planning Guide

COMNAVSURFLANT 4080 series/COMMARFORLANT 4000.10 orders

COMNAVSURFPAC/COMMARFORPAC 4080 series orders

FMFLantO P3120.15A, SOP for MAGTF Deployments

International Air Transportation Association (IATA), International Standards and Recommended Practices

International Civil Aviation Organization (ICAO) Regulations

International Maritime Organization, International Maritime Dangerous Goods Code (IMDG)

ISO Standard 1496-1, Series 1 Freight Containers-Specifications and Testing

ISO Standard 6346, Freight Containers Coding, Identification, and Marking

MIL-HDBK 774, Palletized Unit Loads

Military Specification MIL-C-1283E, Auxiliary Fuel Cans

MTMCTEA PAM 700-4, Vessel Characteristics for Ship Loading

NAVSWC TR 91630, ESQD Arcs for Maritime Prepositioning Ships

Non-US Government/Foreign Military Sales Rates

US Government, DOD Airlift Rates

US Government, Non-DOD Airlift Rates